Globalization and the Physical Environment

The New Global Society

Globalization and the Physical Environment

Ho-Won Jeong
George Mason University

Foreword by
James Bacchus
Chairman, Global Trade Practice Group
of Greenberg Traurig, Professional Association

Introduction by
Ilan Alon, Ph.D.
Crummer Graduate School of Business
Rollins College

CHELSEA HOUSE
P U B L I S H E R S
A Haights Cross Communications Company ®
Philadelphia

CHELSEA HOUSE PUBLISHERS

VP, New Product Development Sally Cheney
Director of Production Kim Shinners
Creative Manager Takeshi Takahashi
Manufacturing Manager Diann Grasse

Staff for GLOBALIZATION AND THE PHYSICAL ENVIRONMENT

Executive Editor Lee Marcott
Editorial Assistant Carla Greenberg
Production Editor Bonnie Cohen
Photo Editor Sarah Bloom
Series and Cover Designer Keith Trego
Layout 21st Century Publishing and Communications, Inc.

Library of Congress Cataloging-in-Publication Data

Jeong, Ho-Won.
  Globalization and the physical environment/Ho-Won Jeong.
    p. cm.—(The new global society)
  Includes bibliographical references and index.
  ISBN 0-7910-8191-5 (hard cover)
  1. Human ecology. 2. Globalization—Environmental aspects. 3. Sustainable development.
I. Title. II. Series.
GF13.G46 2006
333.72—dc22

                                                           2005015385

"For Nimmy and Her Many Friends in the Natural World"

—Ho-Won Jeong

Contents

Foreword

by James Bacchus

IT'S A SMALL WORLD AFTER ALL

One reason that I know this is true is because I have a daughter who adores Walt Disney World in my hometown of Orlando, Florida. When Jamey was small, she and I would go to Walt Disney World together. We would stand together in a long line waiting to ride her very favorite ride—"Small World." We would stand together in those long lines over and over again.

Jamey is in high school now, but, of course, she still adores Walt Disney World, and she and I still stand together from time to time in those same long lines—because she never tires of seeing "Small World." She is not alone. Seemingly endless lines of children have stood waiting for that same ride through the years, hand in hand with their parents, waiting for the chance to take the winding boat ride through Disney's "Small World." When their chance has come, they have seen the vast variety of the world in which we live unfold along the winding way as it appears to the child in all of us. Hundreds of dancing dolls adorn an array of diverse and exotic settings from around the world. In the echoing voice of a song they sing together—over and over again—they remind all those along for the ride that ours is a world of laughter, a world of tears, a world of hopes, and a world of fears.

And so it is. So it appears when we are children, and so it surely appears when we put childhood behind us and try to assume our new roles as "grown-ups" in what is supposed to be the adult world. The laughter, the tears, the hopes, the fears, are all still there in a world that, to our grown-up eyes, keeps getting smaller every day. And, even when we are no longer children, even when we are now grown-ups, we don't really know what to do about it.

The grown-up name for our small world is "globalization." Our globalizing world is getting smaller every day. Economically and otherwise, our world is becoming a place where we all seem to be taking the same ride. Advances in information, transportation, and many other technologies are making distance disappear, and are making next-door neighbors of all of us, whatever our nationality, whatever our costume, whatever the song we sing.

When Walt Disney first introduced the "Small World" ride at the World's Fair in New York in 1964, I was in high school, and we could still pretend that, although the world was getting smaller, it still consisted of many different places. But no more. The other day, I took a handheld device, called a "BlackBerry," out of my pocket and e-mailed instructions to a colleague in my law firm regarding a pending legal matter. I was on a train in the Bavarian mountains in Germany, while my colleague was thousands of miles away in the United States. In effect, we were in the same small place.

This is just one example of our ever-smaller world. And, however small it seems to me in my middle age, and however smaller it may become in my lifetime, it is likely to shrink all the more for my daughter Jamey and for every other young American attending high school today.

Hence, we announce this new series of books for high school students on some of the results of globalization. These results inspire hope, shown in the efforts of so many around the world to respond to the challenges posed by globalization by making international laws, building international institutions, and seeking new ways to live and work together in our smaller world. Those results also inspire fear, as evidenced by streets filled with anti-globalization protesters in Seattle, London, and other globalized cities around the world.

It is hard to tell truth from fiction in assessing the results of globalization. The six volumes in this series help us to do so. Does globalization promote worldwide economic development, or does it hinder it? Does it reduce poverty, or does it increase it? Does it enhance culture, or does it harm it? Does it advance the cause of human rights, or does it impede it? Does it serve the cause of workers' rights, or does it slow it? Does it help the environment, or does it hurt it? These are the important questions posed in these volumes. The hope is that in asking these questions the series will help young people find answers to them that will prove to be better than those found thus far by "grown-ups."

I have had the privilege of trying to begin the process of finding some of these answers. I have helped negotiate international trade agreements for the United States. I have served as a member of the Congress of the United States. I have been one of seven jurists worldwide on the court of final appeal that helps the 148 countries that are Members of the World Trade Organization to uphold international trade rules and to peacefully resolve international trade disputes. I am one of these who see far more reason for hope than for fear in the process of globalization.

I believe we will all be more likely to see globalization in this way if we recall the faces of the dancing dolls in Disney's "Small World." Those dolls are from many different countries. They wear many different costumes. But their faces are very much the same. The song they sing is the same. And, in that song, they remind us all that as we all ride together, "There's so much that we share, that it's time we're aware it's a small world, after all." Indeed it is. And, if we remember all that we in the world share—if we remember above all, our shared humanity—then we will be much more likely to make globalization a reason to hope that our smaller world will also be a better world.

James Bacchus
Chairman, Global Trade Practice Group
of Greenberg Traurig, Professional Association
April 2005

Introduction
by Ilan Alon

Globalization is now an omnipresent phenomenon in society, economics, and politics, affecting industry and government, and all other walks of life in one form or another. THE NEW GLOBAL SOCIETY series gives the reader a well-rounded understanding of the forces of globalization and its multifaceted impact on our world. The international flavor is evident in the make-up of the authors in the series, who include one Israeli, one New Zealander, one Bulgarian, one Korean, and two American scholars. In addition to an international slate of authors, many of whom have lived and worked around the world, the writers hail from fields as diverse as economics, business, comparative literature, and journalism. Their varied experiences and points of view bring a comprehensive and diverse analysis to the topics they write about.

While the books were written to stand alone, those readers who complete all six will find many points of commonality between the books and many instances where observations from one book can be directly applied to points made in another.

These books are written for the lay person and include definitions of key terms and ideas and many examples that help the reader make the ideas more concrete. The books are short and non-technical and are intended to spur the reader to read more about globalization outside these books and in other sources such as magazines, newspapers, journals, Internet sources, and other books on the topics. The discussion of the positive and negative aspects of the consequences of globalization, both here and abroad, will allow the reader to make their own judgments about the merits and demerits of globalization.

A brief description of each of the six books in the series follows:

Globalization and Development—Eugene D. Jaffe
Eugene D. Jaffe of the Graduate School of Business, Bar-Ilan University, Israel, and current Visiting Professor at Copenhagen Business School, Denmark, explains the key terms and concepts of globalization and its historical development. Specifically, it ties globalization to economic development and examines globalization's impact on both developed and developing countries. Arguments for and against globalization are presented. The relevance of globalization for the American economy is specifically addressed.

There are many illustrations of the concepts through stories and case examples, photographs, tables, and diagrams. After reading this book, students should have a good understanding of the positive and negative aspects of globalization and will be better able to understand the issues as they appear in the press and other media.

Globalization and Labor—Peter Enderwick
Peter Enderwick is Professor of International Business, Auckland University of Technology, New Zealand, and a long-time researcher on international labor issues. His book provides a discussion of the impact of globalization on labor with a focus on employment, earnings, staffing strategies, and human resource management within global business. Contemporary issues and concerns such as offshore sourcing, labor standards, decreasing social mobility, and income inequality are treated. The book contains many case examples and vignettes illustrating that while globalization creates

both winners and losers, there are opportunities to increase the beneficial effects through appropriate policy.

Globalization and Poverty—Nadejda Ballard

Nadejda Ballard is a professional international business consultant with clients in the United States and Europe and is an adjunct instructor for international business at Rollins College, Winter Park, Florida. In addition to her extensive experience living and working in various countries, Nadejda is also a native of Bulgaria, a developing country that is struggling with many of the issues discussed in her book.

Globalization, which is reshaping our society at all levels from the individual to the national and regional, is also changing the way we define poverty and attempt to combat it. The book includes the ideas of academics and researchers as well as those who are charged at the practical level with grappling with the issues of world poverty. Unlike other books on the subject, her aim is not to promote a certain view or theory, but to provide a realistic overview of the current situation and the strategies intended to improve it. The book is rich with such visual aids as maps, photographs, tables, and charts.

Globalization and the Physical Environment—Ho-Won Jeong

Ho-Won Jeong teaches at the Institute for Conflict Analysis and Resolution at George Mason University and has published *Global Environmental Policymaking*, endorsed by both current and past Executive Directors of the United Nations Environmental Programme. His new book for Chelsea House discusses the major global impacts of human activities on the environment including global warming, ozone depletion, the loss of biological diversity, deforestation, and soil erosion, among other topics. This book explores the interrelationship of human life and nature. The earth has finite resources and our every action has consequences for the future. The effects of human consumption and pollution are felt in every corner of the globe. How we choose to live will affect generations to come. The book should generate an awareness of the ongoing degradation of our environment and it is hoped that this awareness will serve as a catalyst for action needed to be undertaken for and by future generations.

Globalization, Language, and Culture—Richard E. Lee

Richard E. Lee teaches world literature and critical theory at the College of Oneonta, State University of New York. The author believes that globalization is a complex phenomenon of contemporary life, but one with deep ties to the past movements of people and ideas around the world. By placing globalization within this historical context, the author casts the reader as part of those long-term cultural trends.

The author recognizes that his American audience is largely composed of people who speak one language. He introduces such readers to the issues related to a multilingual, global phenomenon. Readers will also learn from the book that the cultural impacts of globalization are not merely a one-way street from the United States to the rest of the world. The interconnectedness of the modern world means that the movements of ideas and people affect everyone.

Globalization and Human Rights—Alma Kadragic

Alma Kadragic is a journalist, a writer, and an adjunct professor at Phoenix University. She was a writer and producer for ABC News in New York, Washington D.C., and London for 16 years. From 1983–89 she was ABC News bureau chief in Warsaw, Poland, and led news coverage of the events that led to the fall of Communism in Poland, Hungary, Czechoslovakia, East Germany, and Yugoslavia.

Her book links two of the fundamental issues of our time: globalization and human rights. Human rights are the foundation on which the United States was established in the late 18th century. Today, guarantees of basic human rights are included in the constitutions of most countries.

The author examines the challenges and opportunities globalization presents for the development of human rights in many countries. Globalization often brings changes to the way people live. Sometimes these changes expand human rights, but sometimes they threaten them. Both the positive and negative impacts of globalization on personal freedom and other measures of human rights are examined. She also considers how the globalization of the mass media can work to protect the human rights of individuals in any country.

All of the books in THE NEW GLOBAL SOCIETY series examine both the pros and the cons of the consequences of globalization in an objective manner. Taken together they provide the readers with a concise and readable introduction to one of the most pervasive and fascinating phenomena of our time.

Dr. Ilan Alon, Ph.D.
Crummer Graduate School of Business
Rollins College
April 2005

1

Introduction: Environmental Changes and Globalization

Paradise Lost

The residents of Playa Cangrejo, an idyllic fishing village near the tropical mountains of the Isthmus of Tehuantepec in Oaxaca, Mexico, have been going through life changes due to the economic effects of globalization. Local fisherman Isaias "Chayon" Seferino Martinez used to go out to catch fish every morning and evening in a small boat to make his living. However, fish began to get smaller and smaller, due to contamination from the Pemex oil refineries at Salina Cruz, a port city located about 20 miles away. Since fishing does not support his living any more, Martinez takes a long bus ride at 5 A.M. to go to work in an electronics store far from his village.

According to local environmentalists and fishermen, Pemex created a negative effect on the marine life and coastlines (Figure 1.1). Martinez said that despite its promise of more jobs, the refinery has created unemployment. Since 90 percent of fresh water is diverted for the refinery, agriculture is not feasible. Fish have been depleted because of polluted water.

The government of President Vicente Fox is pursuing a gigantic project to build a dry canal for international trade in the Isthmus of Tehuantepec in Oaxaca. The dry canal through the Isthmus will be lined with petrochemical operations and mineral excavation, industrial shrimp farms, and eucalyptus plantations. The non-indigenous eucalyptus trees tend to overrun native ecosystems. Cultivating non-native species of shrimp from the Philippines and other areas may push local shrimp fishermen to the edges of viable business with the spread of foreign bacteria.

The industrial farming, land acquisitions, and road building will lead to destruction of the Chimalapas rain forest and the indigenous communities. The four-lane highway project funded by the World Bank will open the jungle to deforestation by the U.S., Canadian, Chilean, Chinese, and other lumber companies, with privatization of indigenous land and displacement of its inhabitants. The delicate rain forests, coastal regions, and the indigenous culture of the Isthmus of Tehuantepec in Oaxaca, Mexico, stand at a critical juncture to be lost forever.

Source: Adapted from Kari Lydersen, "Another Piece in the Puzzle: Plan Puebla Panama: Mexico's Latest Assault on the Environment and Indigenous Culture," *Clamor.* Nov/Dec 2001., Iss.11. Available online at *http://www.clamormagazine.org/issues/11/*.

As the productive engine of the planet, the ecosystem is maintained by the communities of species that interact with each other and

Figure 1.1   A Mexican man looks on as crude oil seeps out of a pile of riverbank sand piled up after the cleanup of a recent oil spill on January 30, 2005. The Mexican state of Veracruz has suffered five spills of crude oil or semi-refined products from the pipelines of the state oil monopoly Pemex in 2005 alone. Pemex's rusting pipelines and poorly maintained infrastructure need extensive repair to avoid such spills.

with the physical setting surrounding them. A viable support system for species consists of mountains, forests, grasslands, rivers, islands, and coastal and deep-sea waters. Humans are just one of tens of millions of living species on the planet whose various features have been shaped through 3.5 million years of evolution.

Healthy ecosystems have worth beyond their market value. The earth would not be habitable without nature's ability to purify air and water, and decompose and recycle nutrients. Ecosystems yield irreplaceable goods and services, from the water we drink to the air we breathe, from the fish we catch in the sea to the wood we harvest in the forest.

Globalization can be defined as the trend towards a single, integrated, and interdependent world. In an environmental context, globalization reflects both the prehistoric and historic tendency of the human species to expand their activities. The relationships between humans and nature were dramatically altered with the agricultural development that may be traced back some 12,000 years. A severe degradation of the earth's overall system has resulted from the processes associated with the rise of human civilization. Local biological diversity has been greatly diminished with the conversion of grasslands and forests for agriculture. Only a few species of agricultural crops and domesticated animals are supported after the loss of the habitat for a great variety of species.

The globalization of the planet, which has proceeded for millennia, is based on the interdependence of human population growth, pursuit of resources, and technology. For most of human history, ecological destruction, as a by-product of human enterprise, remained a localized and limited concern. Population growth and consumption curves were almost flat for the previous hundreds of millennia prior to the Industrial Revolution.

The arrival of an industrial culture at a global scale magnified the human impact on nature. Human beings have changed large chunks of the earth's natural terrain before, yet the increased ability to affect the whole physical and chemical cycles of the planet represents a watershed. Many forms of damage to the earth and its inhabitants grew in severity and scope with the resource extraction required for mass production. In particular, as author James Gustave Speth has noted, it "was not until after World War II that the fast forward button was pushed down and held."[1]

Ecological degradation encompasses global dimensions beyond cultural differences, divided political boundaries, and diverse economic systems. The ability to affect the environment in remote areas has been further intensified by the economic integration and global expansion of production and trade.

Now production processes are flexibly organized regardless of time differences and distance in space. The human impact on the environment is felt everywhere on a planetary scale. The globalization of economic activities has resulted in the modification of all natural systems and cycles.

Globalization has integrated not just distant economies but also remote environments and government policies on how to manage natural resources. In contrast to armed conflicts and human rights violations that may be noticeable only in specific societies, most environmental changes have universal effects in every corner of the planet. In the modern era, the nature of environmental issues in different parts of the world has become similar due to global economic integration and industrialization. Ecosystems have been distorted more in the past 50 years than in any era of history. The turn of the 21st century has brought us across a threshold to a new reality in which nature no longer remains a place free of human control.

ECONOMIC EXPANSION
Remarkable population growth and associated economic activities have overburdened the natural environment. With expansion in the human population, virtually every measure of human society, ranging from the production of goods and energy consumption to the accumulation of waste, is increasing at an astonishing rate (Figure 1.2). Along with a 35 percent increase in the world population, the global economic output has increased by 75 percent for the last 20 years.

Global energy use is up 40 percent from the early 1980s; the use of coal, oil, and natural gas was 4.7 times higher in 2002 than in 1950. Global use of wood for paper, lumber, and other timber products has more than doubled since 1950. As a result of **deforestation** and the increased use of fossil fuel for transportation and factories, carbon dioxide levels in 2002 were 18 percent higher than in 1960, contributing to global warming.

Figure 1.2   The expansion of the human population has drastically accelerated the production of goods and energy consumption.

The expansion of the world economy has to keep up with the material demand of the population poised to grow by another 25 percent over the next 20 years. The world economy is expected to "quadruple in size again by mid-century, just as it did in the last half-century."[2] Along with it, the demand for wood is expected to double and the consumption of fresh water is expected to expand by more than 70 percent over the next half-century.

ECOLOGICAL COSTS

Material gains have not come without a huge cost to the environment. The consequences of an ecological crisis at a global scale are substantial, ranging from rising sea levels, widespread collapse of fisheries, and declining productivity of the soil to destruction of tropical forests and the extinction of species. The magnitude of human-induced changes in terrestrial and marine ecosystems is unprecedented. Nearly all the world's ecosystems have been shrinking, as land has been converted for industrial growth, mining, agriculture, and urbanization.

Forests have been cleared to find minerals, increase grazing land for cattle, or build homes, shopping malls, farms, and factories. More than 97 percent of old-growth forest, forest that has not had significant human disturbance altering its content or structure, is gone. The demand for water has forced many changes to river systems and wetlands. The earth's wetlands, from coastal swamps to inland floodplains, have been drained or filled to increase agricultural land, develop a golf course, or extend an airport runway. About half the mangroves and other wetlands have disappeared. The pace of extinction of plants and animals has been accelerated by not only the destruction of habitats but also the pollution of both the air and water.

Many unknown environmental risks have surfaced from the widespread use of chemicals and inappropriate management of agricultural wastes, causing potential harm to human health. Farm animal waste produces toxic algal blooms, leading to massive fish kills. Many of the new chemicals and radioactive substances can be devastating to all living species even in the most minute quantities.

When chemicals are discharged directly without treatment, they leak and seep into fresh water sources. The chemicals (pesticides, fertilizers, and hormones) contaminate soil, water, and air, poisoning people and killing animals. These chemicals not only wipe out wildlife but also are a major source of human illness.

The earth is choked with poisonous gases mostly from our daily activities like driving cars, warming our houses, and running power stations. Industrialization and deforestation have driven changes in the geochemical cycle of carbon. Carbon dioxide concentration affects world vegetation patterns and climate at a large scale through the effects of global warming. Extreme weather patterns such as heat waves, storms, and floods disturb life-supporting natural systems and human health through spread of infectious diseases.

The increased use of resources is a major driving force behind the large biospheric transformations. In fact, vast parts of the earth are creamed off for human consumption. The planet has been treated as if it "were created explicitly for our pleasure and exploitation, and we could use its boundless resources endlessly, with few consequences."[3] An appalling deterioration of our planetary habitat would not be stopped "merely by continuing to do exactly what we are doing today" even without population and economic growth.[4]

TECHNOCULTURE

Technological innovations of all kinds have increased production efficiency, often by raising the capacity of people and machinery to extract resources. Beneath technoculture lies the assumption that resources are virtually limitless.[5] For instance, efficient agriculture and fishing pose significant threats to the quality of soil and preservation of fish stocks, even though the use of artificial fertilizer and high-tech fishing gear has helped produce more food and catch more fish.

The seas, lakes, and rivers have provided resources for livelihood and sustenance of local communities for millennia. However, the marine and freshwater conditions have been radically changed by a rapid expansion of commercial fishing. Damage to ocean ecosystems and reduced fish yields are inevitable if we consider the fact that today's super-trawler fishing vessels process hundreds of tons of fish per day. Many fishing communities suffered declines following commercial exploitation. As a consequence of dwindling harvests, one in four fish reaching market today comes from fish farms. A fish farm depends heavily on an outside supply of grain and protein meal supplements such as soybeans. Fish farming produces high levels of waste, often with outbreaks of disease and chemical pollution.

There is a trade-off between high commodity production and impaired ecosystem services. While our use of technology has enhanced short-term production, long-term productivity of ecosystems has been significantly undermined. Even if more food can be produced owing to the intensification of agriculture, it can, if not well managed, expose communities to toxic pesticides.

Clearance of forests and filling in wetlands change the quality and quantity of the local biochemical cycles, consequently having a negative impact on economic life. While timber production has supported an increase in the consumption of paper and housing material, deforestation has caused increased downstream flooding, reduced water quality, and sedimentation in rivers and lakes. Industrialization stimulates economic growth, but at the same time, it means increased exposure to heavy metals and toxic chemicals. Rising energy use has fuelled industrial growth, but increased emissions caused air pollution. Smokestack industries generate acid rain, which, in turn, damages forests and wildlife. Severe industrial pollution in parts of Central and Eastern Europe is responsible for many miles of dead and dying trees as well as dead fish in rivers and lakes.

The biosphere does not return to equilibrium once it reaches a certain level of stress. Overexploitation and mismanagement harm an ecosystem's ability to regenerate itself. The size and quality of our natural assets are dwindling. Non-renewable resources such as oil are gone once they are consumed. Even renewable resources are under pressure to be completely depleted. Numerous plant and animal species have been overexploited to extinction, destined to be lost forever.

THE GLOBALIZATION CONTEXT

Globalization trends illustrate not only the diminishing control of the environmental crisis by local communities but also the unequal distribution of the harmful effects. Ecological degradation on a global scale reflects the cumulative effects of many changes in the physical, biological, and chemical processes of a local environment. Desertification as well as air and water pollution can be intensified by geophysical linkages. Complex ecosystems with shared river and lake basins transcend national boundaries, permitting the flow of pollutants both regionally and globally.

Since toxic material moves freely, pollution has been globalized, with increased risks for many local communities; the movement of pollution is not subject to passport control between national borders. Pollution from factories and power stations in North America, Europe, and Russia can enter an ecological system of a remote Arctic region. Thus, in spite of the absence of polluting industries, people living in the Artic region are not free from chemicals. Some chemicals move up from lower to higher stages of the food chain: from plants and fish to seals, whales, polar bears, and humans (Figure 1.3). The breast milk of the Inuit peoples in the Arctic contains chemicals that did not originate in the region.

Different parts of the world are interconnected through atmospheric changes such as global warming and depletion of the ozone layers. The patterns of weather changes in the tropical waters of the South Pacific are closely linked to natural events at the frozen end of the planet. The small islands at the equator will be the first to submerge underwater with the melting polar glaciers, ice sheets, and snow covers.

Rising energy use remains as one of the main causes of global warming, and such countries as the United States and China contribute heavily to emission of the large proportion of greenhouse gases. Although the greenhouse effect is globally felt, the severity of regional and local impacts varies. Excessive burning of fossil fuels may derive from intensive industrial activities that contribute to national economic growth in one country, but negatively affects the welfare of people in other countries. The destruction of tropical rain forests for farming

Figure 1.3   These polar bears come onto the land in great numbers at Churchill, Manitoba, in the early summer to wait for the sea to freeze again later in the fall. Though their environment may seem pristine to us, in fact, as a predator at the top of the food chain, their body concentrates toxins that come from the worldwide environment.

and extraction of minerals is motivated by regional economic interests, but its effect via climate changes is global. One region of the world, or even a continent, is not immune to the environmental consequences of a major disaster.

Ecological globalization in many guises presents difficult challenges not easily resolved in a traditional governance system. The globalization of an **environmental conflict** is characterized by an asymmetric relationship between victims and polluters. Ecological relationships are imbalanced because the harmful effects are not distributed according to the level of contribution to the pollution. People living in the low-lying islands in the South Pacific, who have a minimum level of fossil fuel consumption, will pay a heavy price for the continued rise in atmospheric temperatures. In global warming, the polluters are such powerful countries as the United States, Russia, and China who often ignore the concerns raised by small island countries that suffer most from consequences such as a rising sea level.

ECONOMIC GLOBALIZATION

Many of nature's products are consumed directly without ever passing through a market. Many indigenous and local people rely on them for survival. Little or no monetary value is attached to natural services provided by clean air, water, and forests in an increasingly market-driven global economy. On the other hand, trade-related pressures such as competition for cheaper prices contribute significantly to pollution and deterioration in natural resource bases. Increased international trade promotes business of all sorts that even include transfer of toxic materials from industrialized countries to developing ones.

Whereas cheaper goods are often prioritized over better environmental quality in a free market economic system, social costs increase with the irresponsible use of collective resources such as air and water. The profit motive in a free market economic system does not count ecological values, since monetary calculations alone determine the choice of the means for production. An emphasis on enhancing efficiency and productivity results in the neglect of the social and ecological costs of polluting water and air. When material interests override ecological concerns, short-term economic gains are achieved at the expense of long-term environmental stability.

Economic globalization tends to lead to an expansion of environmentally destructive growth and a decrease in the ability of national governments to regulate environmental challenges, as well as an increase in corporate power. The stimulation of particular sectors like transportation and energy brings about negative environmental side effects. Ecological destruction is a sign of the imbalance in the way our industrial civilization sets its priorities and governs itself. Environmental concerns are not given priority in many Third World countries that not only face such a pressing need for survival as food and energy but also struggle to achieve financial and monetary stability. For instance, logging rain forests has been used as an exportable means of exchange by debt-laden Third World governments.

Many large-scale development projects erode the economic and ecological bases of local populations, as is illustrated by infrastructure projects criss-crossing the Amazon. These projects encompass construction of new railroads, highways, river channels, hydroelectric dams, and gas and power lines. Once these projects are completed, between 30 and 40 percent of the region will likely be deforested or heavily degraded. Instead of mining, logging, land speculation, and soybean agriculture, environmental groups suggest that populations engage in sustainable development such as high-value agro-forestry, perennial crops, and low-impact forestry in designated areas and eco-tourism.

Even though environmental deterioration increases with growth in the global economy, the means to reduce air pollution and acid rain has not been sufficiently developed. Downward pressures on the local ecological systems can be countered by making international investment conditional on a demonstrated commitment to environmental protection. Speeding economic growth poses challenges in the efforts to slow environmental degradation.

Sustainable development is necessary to integrate economic and environmental policies. We need to preserve the water resources and utilize renewable energy. It is an illustrative example that the United Arab Emirates, one of the major oil-exporting countries, has been involved in research on a new generation of solar panels as part of their commitment to reducing the flaring of gases from onshore and offshore oilfields and exploring clean energy from the sun.

CONSUMERISM AND THE FREE MARKET ECONOMY

Powerful anti-environmental forces existed prior to the full scale of globalization. However, evolving patterns of consumerism and production have contributed to a new level of environmental deterioration. Consumption has been stimulated by lower prices of many commodities that have been made available, in part, with wages as low as a few pennies per hour. A globalizing world has also allowed large corporations to look across national borders to extract resources more easily as well as find a market to sell their products.

Consumerism represents the symbols of modernity and the expansion of a market economy. As author Gary Gardner has written, "From fast food to disposable cameras and from Mexico to South Africa, a good deal of the world is now entering the consumer society at a mind-numbing pace."[6] The consumer culture has been promoted by the 100 percent increase of global advertising over the past 20 years.

The common lifestyle and culture of Europe, North America, and Japan is going global in the 21st century. More than 1.7 billion members of the consumer class are believed to exist today, with nearly half of them in the developing world. The number of consumers has expanded with the transition of most countries toward a market economy. Even the remaining pockets of socialist countries, notably Cuba and North Korea, are expected to move toward a market economy.[7]

The levels of consumption currently held by several hundred million of the most affluent people cannot be replicated by the majority of others without causing a severe crisis in climate, biological diversity, air quality, water supply, and forests. Even the current level of consumption may have to be reduced due to dwindling global resources. According to the June 2004 issue of *National Geographic*, the demand for oil, at a current consumption level of 80 million barrels a day, cannot be sustained for more than two decades. The production of easily extracted oil is expected to peak somewhere between 2016 and 2040, but it will be followed soon by a rapid decline.

The number of motor vehicles in the world has increased from 50 million in 1950 and 250 million in 1970 to 500 million today. It is expected to rise to over 800 million by 2010, with the production of 100,000 new cars every day. More pressure will be put on the environment with the increase in material flow needed to make all those cars and the disposal of worn-out ones, as well as the fuel supply for running them.

Automobiles represent higher social status and increased mobility for the emerging class of consumers in rapidly industrializing countries such as China. China is currently the world's fastest growing auto market. The number of cars in China has been rapidly accelerating, for instance, with about 1.8 million cars sold in 2003 alone. The current growth rate suggests China will have 150 million privately owned cars (more than all the cars in the current world) by 2015. If and when the car ownership there reaches U.S. proportions, China will boast 600 million cars. Massive investment by foreign companies has been attracted in a rush to meet the new demand.[8]

ENVIRONMENTAL POLICIES AND ACTION

Given their dominant role, humans cannot escape the responsibility of managing their impact on nature. Even though we are destroying our local ecosystems, we are still part of the global system. The continued survival of our species depends on the health of this system. The world's top scientists, including a majority of Nobel scientists, made a plea to recognize that the earth's ability to minimize the effects of destructive consumption and to absorb waste is finite.[9] If we understand the earth's limited capacity and its fragility, we can no longer ravage it. This ethic needs to motivate the public and reluctant governments to adopt the needed changes.

Efforts can be made to raise car and truck fuel efficiency as well as to develop renewable energy. In the transportation sector, gasoline-electric hybrids have already been introduced to the market. Through phased increases in taxes on oil and gasoline consumption, fuel prices can reflect environmental and other costs. Higher taxes on fossil fuels and tax incentives for switching to more renewable energy sources can be combined with the reduction and elimination of worldwide subsidies on oil, coal, and gas.

In order to achieve higher energy efficiency, we need to cut energy consumption per unit of production and switch over to solar and thermal energy. Cutting-edge "green technologies" can be applied to renewable energy production based on solar cell manufacturing and wind turbines. Solar cells can generate electricity for many of the 2 billion people living in rural Third World communities.[10] As author Jean-Francois Rischard notes, "Very thin wallpaper-like solar panels could turn almost any large object into a power station, and fuel cells could act as storage devices to offset the variability of solar power."[11]

Wind power has more efficiency than coal-fired electricity generation. The deployment of about 250,000 new wind energy turbines in the United States can remove the need for almost two-thirds of coal-fired electricity generation. In Europe, wind power has already emerged as a rapidly growing component of energy systems. In 2001, Denmark generated 15 percent of its energy from wind, an amount that is expected to grow to 30 percent in the near future.[12]

An increase in consumer awareness and choices will encourage sustainable business practice. The environmentally friendly redesign of products along with less packaging can help corporations save money while conserving resources. The demand of corporate accountability can be backed up by consumer campaigns, boycotts, and shareholder advocacy. The reuse and recycling of consumer products, such as televisions, refrigerators, ranges, and computers, will significantly reduce the costs of waste management. Some of the above measures have been tried before here and there, yet it is a matter of resolve by a critical mass on the global scale.

CHAPTER OVERVIEW

Human activities related to increasing production and consumption have accelerated deforestation, dwindled fisheries, and depleted other resources as well as caused pollution. This book examines environmental deterioration in many parts of the globe, discusses the impact of economic activities on ecological balance, and explores strategies to preserve nature and reduce pollution. Globalization has accelerated the process of ecological changes through expanded economic activities and transformed the relationships between nature and local communities.

In Chapter 2, Changes in the Physical Environment, we look not only at the causes and effects of global warming and ozone depletion, but also at changes in the oceans and polar regions. Chapter 3, Loss of Biodiversity, focuses on the alarming rate of species extinction, destruction of rain forests and depletion of fisheries. Many species, vital to balancing the planet's physical and biological systems, are disappearing due to the destruction of their habitats, hunting, overharvesting, and so on. In Chapter 4, Environmental Scarcity and Conflict, we see how resource competition derived from water shortage, desertification, and soil erosion can generate a cycle of conflict with the migration of populations.

The focus of Chapter 5, Ecological Footprint, is on the limited capacity of nature to support human activities. In Chapter 6, Cleaner Production and Consumption, we look at nature's finite ability to assimilate human waste and continuously supply raw materials. More importantly, we examine recycling and methods of production and consumption to reduce waste. In Chapter 7, Sustainable Development, we explore how poverty and inequality interact with degraded environmental conditions. The earth's long-term capacity to support life is undermined by the failure to preserve and properly manage natural resources.

Chapter 8, Global Environmental Agreements, explores how building consensus on global action is necessary to reduce global warming, ozone depletion, and species extinction. International agreements serve as instruments to provide a common framework of action. Chapter 9, Global Institutions and Civil Society, stresses that the implementation of environmental policies requires the participation of diverse actors ranging from non-governmental organizations and national governments to international organizations. Chapter 10 outlines some of the choices for future generations. Throughout, the book illustrates various characteristics of ecological degradation, its effects on human civilization, and efforts made to control a negative impact of economic activities on nature.

Changes in the
Physical Environment

The earth is comprised of the geosphere (rocks, oceans, rivers, lakes, the atmosphere, soils, and ice) and the biosphere constituting the earth's integrated life support system. The ecosystem is threatened by global warming, depletion, and pollution of the sea. The living conditions for humans and other species on the planet have been dramatically affected by soil erosion, deforestation, and the destruction of wildlife habitats.

CLIMATE CHANGE: GLOBAL WARMING

It has been confirmed for the last 30 years by impressive scientific research that the earth is warming up faster than at any time in history. The Intergovernmental Panel on Climate Change (IPCC), sponsored by the World Meteorological Organization and United

Nations Environmental Programme, estimates that the earth would experience the greatest warming in 10,000 years with a temperature increase of 2.0 to 5.8° C by 2100. The rising earth's atmospheric temperature is attributed to man-made emissions of carbon dioxide (CO^2) and other greenhouse gases.

The climbing global temperature shows adverse effects on human life with expanding warm water following the collapse of massive Antarctic ice shelves and dozens of melting ancient glaciers from the Andes to Montana's Lewis Range (Figure 2.1). The rise of the sea level by 50 centimeters (equivalent to 19.8 inches) would easily flood low-lying deltas and coastal areas, and submerge small islands beneath the waves.[13] Millions of people would be displaced from their homes as a result of deadly flooding. Some small Alaskan villages such as Shishmaref have already been encroached by sea waves that move inland with an average of 3 meters (the equivalent of 10 feet) every year.

Rising temperature associated with global warming will also cause prolonged drought and water shortage. The rising

Tuvalu

Located just south of the equator, and west of the international dateline, Tuvalu's nine small atolls and reef islands are not much above sea level. As geographically flat islands, they cannot move away from the coastlines since neither a continental interior for relocation, nor a high interior, is available on a volcanic island. Rising sea levels threaten all the land inhabited along coastlines.

Due to the increasing incidence of wave washover during storms or periods of strong tidal activity, the nine islands of Tuvalu will become uninhabitable within the next 50 years and eventually will be erased from the face of the earth. Annual high tides are creeping further ashore with frequent crop damage from previously unseen levels of saltwater intrusion. Many researchers believe the rising water level is due to climate change caused by global warming.

Source: Saufatu Sopoanga, "Stop My Nation Vanishing," Special Theme Issue: Seas, Oceans and Small Islands, *Our Planet*, 2004.

Figure 2.1   Global warming is having an effect on Antarctic ice shelves and dozens of glaciers from the Andes Mountains to Montana's Lewis range. Shown is Grand Pacific Glacier in Glacier Bay, Alaska. The consequent rise of sea level due to glaciers melting will have effects on coastlines around the world.

planetary surface temperature is illustrated by the observation of 19 of the 20 hottest temperatures over the last two decades.[14] Lethal heat waves never seen before were experienced in Europe and Asia. The hotter temperature causes plant and animal extinction through habitat change as well as threats to human health with increases in waterborne diseases and mosquito-borne diseases such as malaria.

Beyond warming up the earth, atmospheric change would generate freak weather conditions. Thinning sea ice and glaciers in the Artic result from rapid warming, causing changes in the patterns of ocean circulation and vital currents like the Gulf Stream. This, in turn, influences global climate patterns with more intense and frequent natural disasters, including storms, tornadoes, hurricanes, torrential rains, and ice storms.

One of the worst scenarios would be, paradoxically, the arrival of another ice age in northwest Europe. Such an event would be produced by water flowing south from the melting Arctic ice caps, slowing or even cutting off the warm Gulf Stream current. Plummeting land temperatures would follow the influx of cold water, freezing major rivers. Such extreme changes would alter life in northwestern Europe, having a severe impact on crop yields.

Causes of Global Warming

Global warming, associated with the greenhouse effect, is caused by the accumulation of mostly carbon dioxide and other gases such as methane and nitrogen oxide in the atmosphere. The increased level of carbon dioxide causes the earth's heat to be trapped instead of re-radiated into space. Thus, the world's atmosphere functions like the glass of a greenhouse. According to the Intergovernmental Panel on Climate Change (IPCC), greenhouse gases like carbon dioxide are now at record levels in the atmosphere. Once global warming has begun, it will not be easily reversed or even stopped on any reasonable time scale, since it takes hundreds of years for large bodies of water and ice to respond to changes in temperature.

Human pressure on the global climatic system is largely derived from economic activities that have increased the emission of greenhouse gases into the atmosphere. Fossil fuels are the dead remains of animals and plants turned into coal, oil, and gas after being pressed underground for millions of years. Burning fossil fuels in automobiles, factories, and power stations releases the carbon in coal, oil and gas.

About two-thirds of the planet's excess carbon comes from factory smoke and car exhaust emissions in the atmosphere. It is also increased by the destruction of the world's forests that have the capacity to remove carbon naturally from the atmosphere. A reduction in high levels of a heat-trapping greenhouse gas in our atmosphere has become more difficult due to a decrease in the number of trees, which can absorb accumulated carbon dioxide.

The use of fossil fuels has increased by more than 50 percent since 1965, and more carbon is currently released than is absorbed by the planet. Without a dramatic cut in global emissions, atmospheric concentrations of the greenhouse gases are expected to double or may even triple pre-industrial levels at some point in the 21st century.[15]

Continuing growth in total carbon dioxide emissions, accounting for the largest shares of greenhouse gases, has been observed in most regions except Europe. The biggest release of man-made greenhouse gases comes from the United States, followed by China, whose emission level is rapidly increasing. Advanced European countries have been making efforts to reduce greenhouse gas emissions by implementing stricter regulations in the energy sector. However, any cuts made by other countries will be easily dwarfed by a lack of action by China, which is the second biggest emitter.[16]

OZONE LAYER DEPLETION

All life on earth would cease to exist without the ozone layer, a region of the atmosphere about 10 to 25 miles (15 and 50 kilometers) above the earth's surface. Humans, animals, and plants are exposed to the damaging effects of ultraviolet (UV) radiation from the sun. The ozone layer absorbs excessive ultraviolet radiation from the sun before it reaches the ground.

Thus, the ozone layer protects the earth from solar heat by functioning like a sunshade. The ozone layer above the Antarctic has become thin and has a large hole. A higher rate of lethal mutations in humans, animals, and plants is attributed to the rapidly disappearing ozone layer over highly populated areas. Breaks in the protective ozone layer of the atmosphere allow the penetration of harmful UV radiation that can cause skin cancer and eye cataracts. Excessive sunburn experienced by children increases the chance of developing malignant melanoma, the most deadly kind of skin cancer, later in life.

One cause of destruction of the ozone layer was found to be chlorofluorocarbons (CFCs), which are used in cooling devices such as freezers and air conditioners. CFCs and ozone-depleting substances remain for 100 years or more, each molecule acting and reacting repeatedly to break down the ozone.[17] Worldwide efforts have been made to phase out the use of CFCs and other damaging substances to restore the ozone layer gradually.

POLAR REGIONS

The polar regions, the Arctic and Antarctica, have a profound effect on biological diversity as well as world ocean circulation and climate control. Weather patterns can be changed by the release of huge amounts of water into the oceans resulting from the rapid melting of giant ice shelves. Wildlife has been threatened by deforestation and damage to pipelines carrying oil and gas across the Arctic tundra. Arctic marine life is also disturbed by **overfishing** and hunting as well as constant pollution by modern means of transportation such as snowmobiles, ships, and airplanes.

With its plentiful krill and plankton, the Southern Ocean of Antarctica supplies the staple diet for many fish species and whales. Antarctica, with a landmass as large as the United States and Mexico combined, is believed to have abundant mineral resources. Gold, silver, and uranium are believed to be buried offshore, while oil reserves lie beneath the Antarctic Peninsula. Attention has been drawn to regulating access to the common resource domain.

OCEANS

As the planet's last great wilderness, the oceans constitute three-quarters of the planet's surface; their astonishing features include depths that are greater than the height of the world's tallest mountains. The oceans are central to the life-sustaining processes of our planet by controlling natural and atmospheric systems.

More specifically, they shape the global climate by redistributing heat and water as well as absorbing carbon dioxide and other gases. It is believed that basic life forms originate in the seas, dating back to some 550 million years; given the existence of more diverse forms of life at sea than on land, many new species may yet be discovered in the ocean depths.

The world's oceans have supported human existence by feeding billions of people and supplying mineral resources. Careless, unregulated pollution raises concerns about the progressive destruction of this common asset. For years, waste and chemicals have been dumped into the seas with very little thought about the eventual consequences. The management of the oceans has become an international concern.

COASTAL HABITATS

Today's coastal habitats are in danger of destruction from pollution, resource exploitation, and other hazardous human activities. Coastal development has been one of the main factors behind destruction of critical habitat for valuable fish species. Seventy-five per cent of all sea pollution is caused by land-based human activities.

Tropical coastal mangroves have been destroyed to make way for urban development, tourism, and shrimp aquaculture, losing critical nursery grounds for fish and other species. Ever-increasing economic activities have allowed oil, grease, and toxic pollutants to flow into coastal waters. Pollution, resulting from agricultural run-off, fossil fuel burning, and human waste, poses a serious threat to coastal biological diversity.[18]

The loss of coastal wetlands and other important waterways is also accompanied by damage to habitat-rich coral reefs from increased temperatures. Corals are bleached by warmer waters and other effects of global warming, which have a severe effect on reefs. Warming and rising waters are killing coral reefs in the Caribbean, Indian, and Pacific oceans, causing the erosion of beaches (Figure 2.2).

Figure 2.2   Coral reefs serve as the habitats for over 3,000 species. Many of these reefs are thousands of years old. They are vulnerable to pollution, the collecting of species for sale, and overuse by tourism, as well as ocean warming that damages them.

Coral reefs serve as the habitat for well over 3,000 species, from minute shrimp to fish weighing more than half a ton. Many coral reefs are thousands of years old and are regarded as the rain forests of the sea. They support one-fourth of all marine fish and many exotic species (such as sea horses, angelfish, trigger-fish, and huge giant clams). If all the coral reefs in the world were put together, they would be bigger than the landmasses of Asia, Africa, Europe, Antarctica, and North America combined.

While a reef has a massive, rocky structure, it can be easily damaged by pollution, commercial collection of coral, and care-less management of tourism (such as increases in trash and waste as well as boats and anchors breaking off chunks of the reef). Currently approximately 60 percent of the world's coral reefs are under medium to high threat of disappearing. Destruction has ruined some 50 percent of the world's coastal mangroves that are vital nursery grounds for countless species.

Marine life and vital coastal habitats are plagued by increasing pressure from oil spills and marine litter, overfishing, uncontrolled coastal development, and land-based pollution. We have reached a crossroad where the cumulative effect of our exploitation of the ocean significantly diminishes the ability of marine ecosystems to produce the economic and ecological goods and services that we desire and need.

SMALL ISLAND STATES

Small island states are some of the most beautiful places on earth, but they also are particularly vulnerable to natural disasters, like storms, droughts, and floods, which have increased with global warming. The Caribbean was hit by a hurricane outside the normal season while high tides swept Pacific island states. Storms and droughts are expected to grow both in frequency and in severity with global warming. Island inhabitants, surrounded by the seas, are often short of fresh water, given unpredictable rainfall. A global sea-level rise resulting from climate change is the greatest danger of all to these small islands. The estimated sea-level rise in the southwestern Pacific by the range of 1 and 2 millimeters per year would force nearly all of Maldives' 1,196 coral islands to disappear from the map.

Without a dramatic and rapid cut in the worldwide volume of greenhouse gas production, low-lying islands will submerge beneath the waves, turning the entire population into refugees.[19] Ironically, island states contribute the least to a global climate change and sea-level rise, but suffer most from their adverse effects of greenhouse gas emissions produced mostly by industrialized and rapidly industrializing countries. Dependent on the oceans, small islands are also affected by such threats as marine pollution and overfishing of the world's oceans that have led to a decline in their vital fish catches.

Loss of Biodiversity

The earth does not belong to man; man belongs to the earth. All things are connected, like the blood that unites us. Man did not weave the web of life; he is merely a strand in it. Whatever he does to the web, he does to himself.

—The Native American leader,
Chief Seattle of the Suquamish, 1854

Living organisms (plants, animals, and microorganisms) constitute part of ecological processes. The sheer variety of life on our planet supports each other within an ecosystem that includes a unique mix of air, water, and soil. The existence of diverse numbers of species improves an ecosystem's productivity and increases its ability to withstand environmental strain.

The abundant forms and variability of living organisms have gone through evolution over the past 3 million years. The enormity of the interrelations among all elements of ecosystems has not been fully grasped, as they are so vast and complex. **Biological diversity** (also called **biodiversity**) is characterized by the existence of the rich variety of life forms in nature and their essential interdependence.

Even though some 1.75 million species have been scientifically recognized, biologists estimate the existence of at least 12.5 million or more unrecorded species. Only 1 percent of earth's 250,000 plant species and a far less percentage of its animal species have been thoroughly researched. Many species were already lost even before their discovery, and the threat of extinction of many more of the world's animals and plants has never been greater.

The more species exist, the better off are the biological communities and their surrounding nonliving environments. The accelerating rate of extinction, along with dangerously few populations of many species, may lead to an unraveling of the web of our planet.[20] The extinction of even a small number of species can result in disappearance of many other species with the eventual collapse of the entire ecosystem.

THE VALUE OF BIODIVERSITY

Millions of species are essential to maintaining balance on the planet because of their role in soil decomposition and the circulation of nutrients and atmospheric gases. The preservation of biological balance also helps purify toxins and control harmful microbes. The loss of species, along with the destruction of valuable natural habitat, threatens the basic physical system of the planet, involving the recycling of chemicals in the soil, ocean, and atmosphere. Maintaining the spectacular variety of life is crucial to the balance of the planet and human welfare.

Protecting diverse species is critical to the enrichment of human civilization as well as the maintenance of sustainable economic life. Wilderness protection strengthens spiritual, aesthetic, or ethical aspects of our lives with nature's beauty and healing. Hundreds of new plants are discovered each year. Due to its ability of being thoroughly adaptable to an environment, each species on the planet offers a vast source of useful scientific knowledge.

Beyond forming a liveable environment, wild species provide hundreds of products and food ingredients that humans use and eat every day. Wild species of crops help improve harvests with the offer of new genes that resist disease and pests. In addition, plants, animals, fungi, and microorganisms have been a source of materials for medical therapies. Chemical substances from plants have been synthesized to make drugs that cure serious illnesses. For example, the rosy periwinkle found in the rain forests of Madagascar is the basis of important cancer-fighting drugs.

By destroying wild species, humans significantly reduce the quality of their own lives. The welfare of future generations will be jeopardized with great holes torn in the web of life. Wild species and their genetic variations generate billions of dollars of income for agriculture, medicine, and industry every year. In rural communities, people rely on the earth's biodiversity directly, benefiting from many different natural products for food, fuel, and raw materials. Furthermore, natural vegetation protects and sustains their land and water supplies.

THREATS TO BIODIVERSITY

In general, a species is seen as extinct following its lack of appearance for over 50 years. The extinction of both animal and plant species is now believed to be at least ten times faster than previously estimated. The planet now loses approximately 150 species per day with the annual extinction of more than 50,000.

It is in a stark contrast with the last 600,000 years, when the loss was fewer than 10 species each year. It is alarming that 30 to 50 percent of all species are predicted to become extinct within the next 50 years.[21] Diversity in the planet's life would not be recovered within the 10 million years of the human species' expected lifespan.

Once the species perish, they are gone forever. Species can disappear naturally, but the extinction rate is at least 10,000 times greater than the natural rate. With this alarming rate of extinction, the earth would lose more than half of its species when today's high school students reach middle age.[22] This high rate of extinction continues to increase even faster without intensive conservation efforts and education.

Since dinosaurs disappeared from the planet 65 million years ago, more animals have become extinct due to habitat loss and reckless hunting.[23] The loss of forests directly affects the world's biological diversity, causing the mass extinction of huge numbers of plants and animals. In particular, the fast-disappearing tropical rain forests contain a high level of species diversity. Despite their occupation of only about 6 percent on the earth surface, the world's tropical forests (those remaining in South and Central America, Central Africa, and Southeast Asia) are home to over half the world's species.

A typical area of 4 square miles of rain forest is estimated to hold up to 750 species of trees, 1,500 species of flowering plants, 400 bird species, 100 different reptiles, and 60 amphibians, as well as many as 4,000 species of butterflies and many other insects.[24] The Amazon river basin in South America is believed to have more than 1 million animal and plant species. The forests are destroyed at an annual rate of about 78 million acres equal to an area the size of Poland.[25]

When a rain forest in Indonesia, Malaysia, or Papua New Guinea is cut down, we lose almost 95 percent of the species in an entire forest community in addition to the relationships among the many life forms that we are not even aware of. The disappearing rain forests are homes for 90 percent of all monkeys, apes, and their relatives. The orangutan, a great ape called "jungle man" in the local language, builds nests of branches and twigs, and eats leaves, fruits and insects (Figure 3.1). These apes are greatly threatened by the destruction of their forest homes in Southeast Asian rain forests. The magnificent jaguar has almost disappeared from its traditional habitats of South and Central America.

Figure 3.1   This young orangutan is hanging from a tree in Sumatra, Indonesia, one of the last areas of rain forest large enough to support colonies of orangutans. This is a classic case of habitat destruction as the woods around them are being cut down for wood to export around the world. Rain forests are home to 90 percent of all monkeys, apes, and their relatives.

CAUSES OF EXTINCTION

The decimation of wildlife is mainly attributed to habitat destruction and hunting as well as the introduction of new predators, upsetting the balance of nature. The destruction of biodiversity results from not only the large-scale clearing and burning of forests but also the draining and filling of wetlands for the conversion of wild lands to agricultural and urban uses. Natural migration and feeding routes for such animals as caribou are often blocked after being cut by roads and railways. The loss of resting habitats in coastal areas has disrupted the migration route of North American songbirds such as the hooded warbler. The elimination and fragmentation of forests, grasslands, and wetlands, and the destruction of a desert ecological system, have increased the pressures on the world's wildlife.

With the rapid increase in the world population, more habitats have been destroyed. Trees are cut down; land is cleared for livestock or crops; homes and businesses are built, causing more pollution of the air and water; and wetlands are filled in for housing developments. Destructive practices of overfishing and overgrazing also threaten our planetary biodiversity. The loss or contamination of the habitat is related to modern agricultural practices based on indiscriminate use of pesticides and pollution.

Wetlands for alligators and wading birds are among the most vulnerable habitats following forests. The ivory-billed woodpeckers once thrived in the southern part of the United States, but they died off with the destruction of the forests by loggers, miners, and builders. Within the last 100 years, natural grasslands that once existed in the U.S. Midwest and large parts of Asia, Africa, South America, and Australia have been destroyed, mostly for farming and ranching, leaving little space for the survival of bison, elk, zebras, and kangaroos.

Desert plants such as the saguaro cactus seen in the southwestern U.S. deserts live up to 200 years. The giant cacti provide home, food, and shade for birds such as the North American woodpeckers and other small creatures. They are resistant to droughts, but they cannot easily recover from damage caused by humans. The future of the saguaro is endangered as a result of human encroachment in the desert. Without trees to shelter them, young saguaros are extremely vulnerable.

Endangered species can be saved if the wild places where they live are protected by measures such as the restrictions of buildings and access to roads near their habitats. For instance, saving the Everglades in Florida requires prohibiting building homes and businesses that would change the natural flow of water and put many species in danger.

In addition to the destruction of habitats, unique species in one region of the world can be eliminated through either intentional or accidental introduction of invasive species. The new species bring about changes to the ecosystem by threatening the survival of native species. For example, the release of European zebra mussels in the Great Lakes of North America spread widely and killed the indigenous mussels in the continental waterways. Introduction of the Indian mongoose to Hawaii in the 1880s with the intention of killing rats in sugarcane fields has almost wiped out native ground-nesting birds.

Animals are sometimes killed or hunted to the point of extinction. All species of sea turtles face trouble with the destruction of their nesting grounds and injuries from shrimp nets. Hunters seek their meat and shells and collect their eggs. Crocodiles and snakes are killed for their skins to be used for handbags and shoes. The skins and furs of many species (most visibly the leopard and cheetah) make expensive adornments for those who can afford them. Since their prices go up with scarcity, many rare species are pursued vigorously by poachers.

There are many endangered species that have been hunted to extract commercially valuable parts of their bodies. Tiger bones and organs, as well as rhinoceros horns, are sought for traditional Chinese medicine. The illegal hunting of African elephants was accelerated by the demand for their ivory tusks, which are then carved into jewelry or decorative pieces.

In addition, the desire to have exotic pets has increased the trade in a range of live species, including smaller monkeys and marmosets; parrots and other types of colorful birds; large and small reptiles, especially crocodiles, snakes, lizards and tortoises; many species of tropical butterflies; and even certain snails and spiders (Figure 3.2). The woolly monkey, one of the most endangered mammals, is available in a Brazilian pet market. The Mexican red-kneed, bird-eating

Figure 3.2   This chimpanzee is being kept in a cage either as a pet or as part of an exhibit. Captive conditions can never hope to mimic the conditions of an animal like this in its own environment. Unfortunately, for every live animal, there are usually several that don't make it.

tarantula spider may not withstand the persistent drain in its population, because it is popular as a household pet in certain countries.

DEFORESTATION

The goods and services provided by forests range from food, timber, and medicine to firewood, resins, and vines. They recycle nutrients, control the quality and flow of watersheds, and protect soil. Thus deforestation, the clearing of forested land, contributes to the pollution of rivers and creeks and the loss of wild species. With their ability to hold and use large amounts of water, forests are essential to flood control. By soaking up carbon dioxide and other gases out of the earth's air and recycling them into oxygen, forests reduce global warming. Rain forests are called "the lungs of the earth"; the Amazon rain forest produces 40 percent of the world's oxygen. Forests are also vital to the world's biodiversity by serving as habitats for endangered species. Once tropical forests are cut down, the forests that grow back do not reflect the original genetic diversity.

More than half the earth's tropical rain forests, along with the largest reserves of seasonal forests, have disappeared since the 1950s. The remaining old-growth forests, composed of fully mature trees that have not been disturbed by humans over the trees' lifetimes, are left in Canada and Russia. Tropical areas such as the Amazon, Central Africa, and Southeast Asia

Deforestation in Liberia

An estimated 40 to 45 percent of the remaining Upper Guinean Forest Ecosystem is found in West Africa. As one of the world's biological hotspots, this zone displays many endemic fauna and flora. A significant portion of West Africa's original rainforest cover is still left in Liberia, which is host to at least 2,000 flowering plants, roughly 240 timber species, about 125 mammals, 74 known reptiles and amphibians, over 1,000 insect species, and 950 birds. The most notable are the only remaining population of the Pygmy hippopotamus and forest elephants in West Africa as well as dozens of endangered bird species.

The major threats to Liberia's forests, and the wildlife they sustain, come from the government's desire to tap these resources for quick cash. The sustainability of forest management is further threatened by private operators' practice of felling either undersized trees or more trees than are ecologically viable. In addition to being threatened by salvage logging in proclaimed national forest reserves, endangered and slow-reproducing species are at the further risk of extinction by a lack of regulations and enforcement that allows intensive hunting.

These threats have been aggravated by the interminable poverty of rural Liberians and corrupt local officials who engage in profiteering. The near total lack of awareness and prevailing indifference among the local population to the long-term consequences of current actions leaves little hope of protecting this unique forest ecosystem.

Source: Alexander Peal, "Green Spot in Africa," *Our Planet*. Available online at *http://www.ourplanet.com*.

contain the remaining rain forests. However, almost all these areas are under threat from logging, mining, fuel wood collection, and fires.

Many trees in an old-growth forest are over 120 years old. Because of the high quality of their lumber, they have been targeted by loggers. Some redwood trees are 20 to 30 stories high and weigh as much as 800 school buses (Figure 3.3). While 3,500 years are needed for a seedling to grow to its gigantic size, such a redwood tree can be cut down within 2 hours. These trees are essential for science and medicine as well as serving as a habitat for hundreds of species, including endangered species such as the spotted owl. The yew tree native to the northwestern Pacific Coast of North America has bark used for breast cancer treatment.

Forest fires are used to clear trees for pasturelands or such inappropriate agricultural practice as slash-and-burn cultivation, a method of farming in which the forest is first cleared by cutting and then burned to add nutrients to the soil. Large-scale forest burning is said to contribute to about one-third of the current CO^2 emissions.[26] Large fires in Indonesia and Brazil in 1997 contributed to increase in the atmospheric carbon dioxide (CO^2), while the smoke caused health hazards to the entire population.

The current rate of cutting down the rain forests indicates that the Amazon will be deforested by the end of the 21st century (Figure 3.4). Central Africa includes the world's second-largest area of contiguous forests in the Congo Basin. In addition to bush fires, civil wars and drought in Africa are degrading forests. Despite international efforts to set up reserves, the pressure on forests has been relentless.

With greater mechanization of its processes, logging has increased dramatically over the last two decades. Enormous quantities of timber were wasted through inefficient logging practices, including destruction of immature trees of valued species and varieties with commercially less desirable stocks.

Figure 3.3   The woman standing at the base of this redwood tree gives one a sense of their enormity. Some giant redwood trees are 20 to 30 stories high and take 3,500 years to reach this height.

Figure 3.4   This is what is left when the inappropriate practice known as slash-and-burn levels a rain forest in Brazil. At the current rate of cutting there will be no rain forest in the Amazon region by the end of this century.

In developing countries, hardwood timber is an important export commodity to earn foreign currency. Failure to monitor commercial logging adequately has devastated rain forests in Cambodia, Malaysia, and Indonesia. Destruction of the forests is also attributed to submersion of forests in lakes resulting from the construction of large hydroelectric dams. Thousands of square miles of rain forest in the Amazon have been flooded by the creation of huge reservoirs.

Increased destruction in the rain forests coincides with intensive activities of raising cattle, goats, and other livestock. Rain forests are often cut down for plantations for bananas, rubber trees, cashews, and coffee beans. The conversion of forests to agricultural land and pastures has been accelerated by land resettlement schemes for poor people from over-crowded regions.

Amazon forests, which represent the most ecologically complex vegetative formulations on the planet, have been damaged by government policies to build highways and move settlers, as well as by tax incentives and subsidies to engage in cattle ranching. Clearing land for the ranching and production of export crops has also been an important cause of tropical deforestation in Central America. More than 40 percent of the forest cover was lost, with the number of beef cattle more than doubling.[27]

OVER-EXPLOITATION OF FISHERIES

Some 75 percent of major marine fish species are either depleted or dwindling fast due to overfishing. For the last 50 years, industrial fleets of China, Japan, Russia, India, Chile, and other countries have decimated approximately 90 percent of tuna, marlin, cod, halibut, skate, flounder, sharks, and other predators.[28]

The overexploitation of fish populations jeopardizes their existence and availability for future generations.[29] Fish is caught faster than they can reproduce. Not enough young fish are now being left to breed due to advanced fishing methods that catch up too many fish, both large and small, simultaneously.

An ever-growing number of species are on their way to extinction as a result of unsustainable fishing. The wholesale changes to marine ecosystems were brought about by the extensive use of techniques to progressively fish down food chains. Depletion of high-value, top predator species leads to targeting those lower in the chain.

Destructive fishing practices have led to the discarding of some 18 to 40 million metric tons of unwanted fish. These practices and other threats cause a heavy toll to sea turtles and birds as well as life on the seabed. For example, an estimated 100,000 seabirds per year are snared by the practice of longlining in the Southern Ocean (Figure 3.5).

In longlining, a single line up to 81 miles (130 km) long is set behind the boat. Attached to it are literally thousands of baited

Figure 3.5   Commercial fishing is pushing an ever-growing number of species toward extinction due to unsustainable methods. These methods result in millions of metric tons of unwanted fish being discarded after they are caught. Even seabirds are impacted as 100,000 of them are trapped in longline fishing practiced in the Southern Ocean.

hooks. Some of the baited hooks are eaten not by their intended targets, but by seabirds that are dragged under water and drown.

Overexploitation of most major fisheries effectively changed the immensity of the oceans that once seemed invulnerable. The increasing pressure exerted on the seas by fishing affects the ecosystem beyond the targeted fish stocks. The balance of species is altered by overfishing, driving some species to near extinction. Industrial fisheries have decimated 90 percent of large predatory species in the past 50 years. Whales, dolphins, seals, and polar bears have all been threatened by pollution as well as the overexploitation of marine resources.

Negative consequences for the communities, cultures, and economies that depend on marine resources result from decades of abuse of the oceans. Local fishing communities have long lived in harmony with the environment, producing food for both themselves and surrounding towns. In contrast, large-scale commercial fisheries have overharvested marine resources for countries thousands of miles away. Devastation in sea fishing and its related industries undermines the livelihoods of some 200 million people around the world.

BIODIVERSITY IN FRESH WATER

A complex balance in freshwater ecosystems around the world is threatened with the extinction of freshwater birds, fish, aquatic mammals, inland water crustaceans, and turtle species. Over-harvesting, pollutants that wash in from the land, and the release of foreign species have caused a catastrophic decline in biodiversity in freshwater ecosystems. The populations of species living in freshwater ecosystems, including wetlands, rivers, and lakes worldwide, have been reduced by 50 percent since 1970.

The Amazon and its tributaries along the Equator constitute the largest river system on earth. With its magnitude of nearly 2,302,200 square miles (6 million square kilometers), it is known as the most valuable freshwater biological system. Since Lake Baikal is the oldest and deepest in the world, it has a large variety of freshwater species. Over half of its nearly 2,000 animal species are not found anywhere else in the world. The existence of so many rare, endemic species that evolved over a long period of time is an indication of the age and scale of the lake.[30]

Ecological degradation of freshwater ecosystems stems from human activities that have withdrawn or altered much of the available surface water from wetlands, lakes, or river basins. Freshwater habitats are altered due to building dams and draining wetlands for farming. Dam building has had the biggest influence on the aquatic environment by disrupting the flow of a river system. Some fish need to migrate up rivers to spawn before returning to the sea, but their passage is barred by a dam. In the case of the Colorado River, since water is depleted before reaching the sea, fish species in a lower stream exist only in isolated pockets or completely disappear.

Forty percent of the 25,000 known species of fish live in freshwater ecosystems. Pressure on freshwater ecosystems also comes from overfishing as well as hunting such species as crocodiles and caimans for their meat or skin. Indigenous species can be wiped out by the deliberate or inadvertent introduction of alien species that are either predators, parasites, or competitors of native ones.

For thousands of years, small fish called cichlids thrived in Lake Victoria, also known as Victoria Nyanza, the world's second largest freshwater lake. In the 1970s, a predatory fish called the Nile perch was stocked in the lake to improve the fish stock. Unfortunately, the perch underwent a population explosion and has caused the extinction of more than 300 species of cichlids. The disappearance of cichlids, which eat oxygen-absorbing algae, led to the depletion of the lake's oxygen levels, which in turn reduced fish stock.[31] The approximately 600 endemic freshwater fish species in the lakes of the ancient African Rift Valley have also become very rare or extinct largely due to the introduction of the Nile perch.

Environmental Scarcity and Conflict

Deforestation, soil degradation, desertification, air pollution, and water shortage have contributed to the deterioration of the quality of life for the poor in many developing countries. Insufficient natural resources and inequitable standards of living degrade our social fabric and cause conflict. Threats to the quality of life caused by environmental deterioration increase the probability of social unrest. Competition for scarce resources in overcrowded regions produces a volatile social situation for group conflict. In particular, deteriorating resource bases coupled with rapidly growing populations has exacerbated the existing political tensions.

ENVIRONMENTAL SECURITY
With the recognition that the environment provides a fundamental

life-support system, global environmental changes have become an important common security issue. Population dislocation is an inevitable result of extensive deforestation, desertification, drought, soil erosion, and floods. According to a recent study by the Pentagon, severe droughts, flooding, and violent storms on an apocalyptic scale will force waves of boat people to drift from one country to another. Countries may set up virtual fortresses to keep out millions of migrants who leave land that is flooded by a rise in sea level or is no longer able to sustain crops.

The rapid expansion of deserts into previously habitable land will disproportionately affect the poor and most vulnerable members of society, such as women and children, who are least able to adapt (Figure 4.1). Warmer temperatures, increases in evaporation, and water shortage cause longer periods of droughts, which can have a severe impact on food production. The security of food sources, especially in sub-Saharan Africa, is threatened by environmental factors such as severe land degradation.

Desertification has put approximately 135 million people (the equivalent of the combined populations of Germany and France) at risk of being displaced. Drought is a main contributor to the migration of many of the 12 million people in Brazil's arid and rocky northeastern Sertao region to the urban São Paulo area. Due to soil erosion, between 700,000 and 900,000 people in the rural drylands of Mexico's central region leave their homes every year and seek their living as migrant workers.[32]

Poverty forces hundreds of millions of poor people to plunder forests as well as overgraze land. Rain forests in South America, Southeast Asia, and other parts of the world are cut to maintain exports that support the growing population. It will eventually endanger global living conditions through climate changes.

The livelihood of more than 60 percent of the population in developing countries depends on land and water resources. With the deterioration of environmental resources, the number of

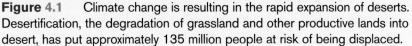

Figure 4.1   Climate change is resulting in the rapid expansion of deserts. Desertification, the degradation of grassland and other productive lands into desert, has put approximately 135 million people at risk of being displaced.

people living on less than $1 a day has been increasing by 10 million every year.[33] Land degradation threatens food security and livelihoods, particularly in Africa. As we will discuss in Chapter 7, reversing these trends with a global shift toward sustainable development serves the world's best economic, security, and environmental interests.

RESOURCE SCARCITY
Rapid population growth pushes economic and natural resource limits. Population increase can result not only in pollution of the seas, depletion of fish, and increasing water scarcity, but also destruction of tropical forests and the biodiversity they contain. British economist Thomas R. Malthus argued two centuries ago that population growth would arithmetically outstrip increases

in the food supply. Over 20 years ago, scientists wrote a book called *The Limits to Growth*, which predicted unstable future trends related to the impact of rapid population growth and consumption of the food supply and non-renewable resources.

Intense industrial activities combined with a growing population will put a severe strain on the ability of this finite planet to sustain economic livelihood and absorb pollution. Disruption and conflict will become endemic, as environmental scarcity and overpopulation may cause frequent wars over basic resources such as oil, food, and water. In a neo-Malthusian interpretation, the world will increasingly face crises and conflicts generated by fast-growing populations competing for declining resources as well as massive urbanization, migration pressures, and reduced government capacity.

Approximately half of the 50 armed conflicts since the end of the Cold War have involved environmental factors in one way or another. In many regions of the world where resources are not able to support the population, efforts to assert or prevent control over water, fertile cropland, and forests create conditions for conflict between and within countries. The water conflict between Israel and its Arab neighbors is related to the use of the River Jordan. Turkey has been building dams on the Tigris and Euphrates rivers, which originate within its borders, to irrigate 4.2 million acres of land, but controlling the flow of these rivers has reduced water available for irrigation for downstream countries such as Syria and Iraq by 40 to 90 percent.[34] In another example, Bangladesh has disputed India's plan to build a dam to divert water from the upper Ganges.

Since good soil and agricultural conditions are not evenly distributed around the world, conflict inevitably arises from competition for limited or inequitably distributed land. Land degradation and deterioration of other resource bases further aggravate the conditions for conflict. In many situations, a poor majority is pushed to the most ecologically vulnerable land, while a wealthy minority controls the fertile land. The struggle for access to land has been one of the main causes of civil war in El Salvador, Nicaragua, and other Central American countries.

In poorer countries, too many people are fighting over too few resources. Those affected by environmental degradation are forced to leave their lands to seek other means of making a living, possibly coming into conflict with those already settled in the areas to which they migrate. The population influx exceeding the capacity of the host environment contributes to group competition, along with unequal access to scarce resources.

SOIL EROSION AND DESERTIFICATION

Land degradation is often derived from deforestation, poor soil and water management, and overuse of fertilizers and pesticides. The remaining land has to produce more food to support an increasing number of people, resulting in its further abuse. Soil degradation and the loss of productivity, in turn, destroy food security and increase poverty.

Soil erosion is not only a cause but also a consequence of poverty. Poverty forces those who depend on land for their livelihood to overexploit it. Thus, land degradation leads in a downward spiral to worsen poverty amongst the world's poorest people searching for sources of food, energy, and housing. Food insecurity is further aggravated by fast-growing populations and an increasing debt, which makes food import unaffordable.

The most common forms of unsustainable land use are derived from overcultivation, deforestation, and poor irrigation practices. Vegetation destruction, combined with excessive use of water, ploughs, and fires, can in a few years erode soil that has taken millions of years to form. Soil recovery from disturbances is very slow, and the quality of the soil further deteriorates with rain and wind erosion. With the reduction of soil productivity, edible plants can be replaced by non-edible ones.

Extreme land degradation and its inability to support any vegetation result in desertification. Soil erosion and damaged vegetation cover reduce the land's natural resilience to recover from climatic disturbances (Figure 4.2). Human activities such as overharvesting and overgrazing have caused the degradation of more than 15 percent of the earth's land, an area bigger than the United States and Canada combined.

In the years 1945 to 2000, more than one-sixth of the world's arable and grazing land was spoiled due to erosion.[35] Every year the world loses some 25 billion tons of soil, reducing its ability

Environmental Exhaustion: The Example of Haiti

The environmental exhaustion of Haiti is symbolized by the once-green hillsides and meadows that have been virtually cleared, leaving only barren land. The environmental destruction has been accelerated by the crush of poverty and the country's rapid population growth. The daily hardship contributes to eroding essential natural resources. Too many people scrape limited natural resources, leaving the country with one of the world's highest rates of deforestation.

Topsoil is lost to erosion, filling rivers with the resulting sediment and diminishing the freshwater resources. The destruction of forests and associated pollution caused waterborne diseases and damage to human health. A loss of agricultural land and water resources pushes rural residents toward overcrowded urban centers. The seeds of discontent and political struggle germinate and grow from this despair.

The average Haitian woman has 4 to 5 children who face bleak economic and environmental prospects. Haiti's population of 7 million is expected to grow by 30 percent in the next 20 years. In the last two decades, 1.3 million people have fled Haiti as a result of land erosion compounded by political unrest.

Environmental degradation caused Haiti's per capita grain production to drop by 50 percent over half a century. Revitalization of rural agriculture as well as family planning and other basic reproductive health services is essential to sustaining life on the island. Restoring biological diversity can lead to support for the rural populations, while the promotion of land reform will give farmers a stake in preserving the quality of the soil.

Source: Hama Arba Diallo, "Regaining Ground." Special Theme Issue: Global Environmental Facility, *Our Planet* (2003).

Figure 4.2   This soil erosion was caused by clearing trees and grazing cattle in Queensland, Australia. More than one-sixth of the world's cultivatable and grazing lands were lost to erosion between 1945 and 2000.

to produce food. Land degradation and desertification are likely to intensify with the continued growth in population and increasing variations in the climate. If the current trends are left unchecked, arable land is expected to shrink in Africa by two-thirds and in Asia by one-third.

Drylands include arid, semi-arid, and dry sub-humid areas. Throughout the world, drylands still provide much of the world's food, in the form of grain and livestock, yet close to one-third of the world's drylands are degraded, thus diminishing the productive land per capita and decreasing food security. The grave environmental consequences encompass major economic and political disruptions such as mass migration along with loss of income. Soil erosion is particularly threatening economic and physical survival.

Soil erosion and desertification undermine the livelihood of 1 billion people with the annual income loss of $42 billion. In Africa alone, an estimated $9 billion is lost from desertification every year, with $42 billion a year lost worldwide.[36] Close to half of Africa is vulnerable to desertification, affecting some 485 million people, putting livelihoods at risk and propelling people to migrate.

SHORTAGE OF FRESH WATER

Water sustains basic human functions such as health and food production. Obtaining a secure source of water is thus an important concern, given its key role in our consumption, production, sanitation, and human settlements. For instance, water availability is critical to food security, since water shortage reduces crop yields. Since nearly half of the world's rivers are seriously depleted and polluted, conflict and tension can arise over transnational water resource issues.

The world water cycle is expected to fail to meet demands in the coming decades, with every continent feeling stress on its water supply. Forty percent of the global population living in some 80 countries faces serious water shortages. With the continuation of the present rate of water consumption, domestic, industrial, and livestock uses are expected to increase at least 50 percent by 2025, leaving two out of three people without enough water to meet their basic needs.[37]

Many parts of Africa and West Asia experience severe droughts and are vulnerable to a serious lack of water availability. The Middle East holds 0.9 percent of the world's water supply, but 5 percent of the world's population.[38] Research by the

Intergovernmental Panel on Climate Change forecasts increasing drought and desertification along with a decrease in rainfall in the already arid areas of Eastern and Southern Africa.

About 1.5 billion people depend upon groundwater for their drinking water supply. However, less than 1 percent of all fresh-water resources, coming from rivers, lakes, ponds, or aquifers, are a usable supply for ecosystems and people. The volume of freshwater resources is approximately 2.5 percent of the total water volume, which amounts to about 1.4 billion km^3. The amount of groundwater extracted annually is estimated to represent about 20 percent of global water withdrawals.

Agriculture accounts for approximately 70 percent of the world's freshwater use. A growing demand for food leads to a heavier dependence on water for irrigation.[39] Industrial use constitutes about 20 percent of global freshwater withdrawals. Sixty to seventy percent of industrial water consumption is devoted to hydropower and nuclear power generation, with the remainder being allocated to manufacturing processes.

Although access to safe drinking water is a basic right for all human beings, 1.1 billion people do not have access to a clean water supply, including groundwater drawn from a protected well, rainwater, or spring. Nearly 1.8 billion people live with-out adequate sanitation.[40] In Asia alone, safe drinking water is available to one in three people with accessibility of hygienic sanitation to one in two.

In developed countries, per capita daily water consumption ranges from 500 to 800 liters, compared with 60 to 150 liters in developing countries.[41] The access of rural and low-income populations to safe drinking water poses a major challenge. When too much water is taken from big underground reservoirs of fresh water, seawater near coasts seeps in, making the fresh water salty and undrinkable.

Fresh water, including groundwater, is considered as part of an integrated system, since all life on the planet is sustained and linked by water. Poor quality fresh water as well as its shortage can give rise to waterborne disease. Rivers are filled with deadly chemicals coming from mining and industrial pollution. Agricultural chemicals, spread over fields, penetrate rivers and lakes. In many poor areas of the world, rivers have also often been treated as if they were garbage dumps or sewers.

Sound water management is crucial to reducing human vulnerability resulting from degradation of water quality and scarcity. More water is taken out than saved in our aquifers all over the world; an overdraft will eventually cause us to be bankrupt. Huge annual water overdrafts occur in North America as well as North Africa, West Asia, India, and China. Humans waste and pollute water recklessly even though nearly all living things on the planet need water. The pollution of water systems by untreated industrial waste and sewage has a dramatic impact on the volume of available, clean water.

Ecological Footprint

As the most successful species on earth, humans have continuously exploited nature to meet their material desires. However, their ability to continue to do so is limited due to the earth's finite resources. It took some 200,000 years for the number of people on the planet to increase from a few thousands to reach one billion in 1804. Increased food production, along with vast improvements in medicine and hygiene, has allowed the human race to more than triple over the last 100 years. The steepest rise occurred in the 20th century, tripling from 2 billion in 1927 to 6 billion in 1999. In 2002, the world population was increasing by two people per second.[42]

The rapidly expanding human population has led to a parallel increase in consumption. While the level of consumption has been accelerated by technological advance and economic expansion, a large scale of production over-reaches itself, threatening the key resources on which we rely. Human pressure on the world ecological systems far surpasses the changes that all other living species combined can make in nature. In this chapter, we will assess the limited capacity of nature to support human consumption and other economic activities through the concept of the ecological footprint.

CARRYING CAPACITY

The earth's resources can only support a limited number of people. Rapid population growth puts stress on the planet's ability to renew its resources. Having more people without reduction in a consumption level per capita simply means increasing pressure on a wide variety of environmental systems. Carrying capacity is defined in terms of the maximum population size that can be supported in a given environment. A growing population and dwindling natural resources can lead to an excessive carrying capacity.

Nature's ability to satisfy an ever-increasing demand for more resources is limited. Dwindling natural resource bases are well indicated by the decline in per capita production of several basic commodities since the late 1960s. The planet is gradually moving toward overloading the carrying capacity with a rapidly growing population. In particular, Asia has 71 people per square mile of land, far higher than the world average of 17 people per square mile.[43]

The massive overexploitation of our dwindling natural resources will be inevitable without stabilization of the world population. Rapid population growth puts stress on the planet's ability to renew its resources. In many Third World countries, the population increase outstrips economic growth, with the consequence of declining per capita income and deteriorating living standards. During the increase of the world population from 2.5 billion in 1950 to 6 billion in 2000, about 95 percent of the population growth came from the developing world.

Less industrially developed countries account for more than three-quarters of the world's population, while earning only 15 percent of the global income.

Prevailing economic activities are averse to the efforts to reverse the trend toward resource depletion. Present consumption and production seriously hamper the long-term ability to support the global resource bases. Economic growth ought to be adjusted to the earth's carrying capacity. Requirements for the preservation of natural resources should be considered along with economic efficiency.

ECOLOGICAL FOOTPRINT ANALYSIS

Our everyday consumption leaves a mark, like a footprint in the sand, just as eating sandwiches or buying sneakers changes the physical world. Every small change that we make in our daily life is added to an individual ecological footprint. An **ecological footprint** is a measure of how much land and water is needed to produce the resources we consume and to dispose of the waste we produce. In measuring the footprint, we need to know the amount of land and water that is used for producing food, energy, and other necessary materials. For example, the production of 100 pounds of beans might require 1 1/2 acres of arable farmland. We also need to calculate resources used to produce energy, transportation, and packaging that have been involved in bringing the beans to market.

Ecological footprint analysis helps us quantitatively assess the biologically productive area needed for maintaining our life.[44] In addition to the resource demand, thus, ecological footprint includes necessities to absorb the waste of a given population's specific activities, including the garbage we throw away and the carbon dioxide we exhale. In order to lower an ecological footprint, activities such as recycling need to be encouraged to reduce energy and landfill space demand. Since the value of nature is mostly considered in terms of goods and services needed for humans, unfortunately, the concept of species extinction is not seriously incorporated in estimating the footprint.

Resource consumption and waste output can be compared with nature's renewable and regenerative capacity. The ecological surplus or deficit is calculated by subtracting the ecological footprint from nature's capacity that represents the amount of productive land and water areas. A surplus (a positive number) indicates that a population is living within its country's ecological capacity. A deficit (a negative number) shows that a population's material demand is exceeding nature's ability to support it. By using more than our share of resources, we diminish the very capital that sustains current and future generations. The renewable and non-renewable land areas need to be effectively utilized for a given population to exist in a sustainable manner.

How to Measure An Ecological Footprint

Municipal or local footprint data include not only the usage of natural gas, gasoline, and diesel fuel, but also the number and types of vehicles and road miles. The local data also involve housing characteristics and waste and recycling tonnage, as well as acreage and types of land. Since people use resources from all over the world, the footprint methodology adds up the cropland, grazing land, forests, fishing ground, water withdrawals, and energy use that have been used for consumption by the urban population, whichever part of the planet they originate from.

The amount of land needed for each specific economic activity varies. On the basis of measuring humanity's use of nature, footprint analysis helps us explore where the greatest potential for progress toward sustainability can be achieved. For instance, bicycles are the most sustainable, requiring only 1,300 square feet per cyclist, compared with 3,200 square feet needed by buses per passenger and 16,000 square feet per passenger required by cars (Figure 5.1). Overall, the ecological footprint serves as a tool in making decisions on transportation, sprawl, zoning, open space preservation, and environmental preservation.

THE GLOBAL ECOLOGICAL FOOTPRINT

The global ecological footprint can be compared to global acres of biologically productive space, the amount that contributes to the total available natural capital and services. The world's

Santa Monica's Footprint

The city of Santa Monica, located in the county of Los Angeles, California, initiated an ambitious Sustainable City Program that serves as a concrete example of how a community can think, plan, and act in a more sustainable manner. The City of Santa Monica has earned its reputation as a leader in the sustainable community movement. The city's residents supported practices and policies designed to decrease fossil fuel use, reduce pollution, and increase green space.

The energy component of Santa Monica's total ecological footprint has been reduced since 1990. Various innovative programs, initiated by community members and elected officials, have helped a decrease in the overall category of natural gas and diesel fuel use along with increased reliance on the mix of renewable (solar, wind, and geothermal) energy. Dependence on fossil fuel-powered vehicles has been reduced through the increasing use of solar or electric vehicles as well as the promotion of public transportation.

Increased recycling rates also resulted in reducing the city's ecological footprint. Potential energy use has decreased by about 50 percent through recycling glass, paper, plastic, and metal and diverting these materials from landfills. Innovative disposal programs are necessary to further diminish the total waste stream.

Despite the high level of dedication, not all the trends are entirely favorable. In particular, the City of Santa Monica's 2002 Status Report indicates that a booming local economy has put significant burden on transportation, energy, and land use in the residential and commercial sectors, along with an increase in material consumption and waste generation.

Source: Redefining Progress (2004), "Santa Monica's Ecological Footprint 1990–2000." Santa Monica, CA: Environmental Programs Division. Available online at *www.ci.santa-monica.ca.us/environment/index.htm.*

Figure 5.1   A man rides his bicycle to take his geese and chickens to the market in Chengdu, Sichuan, China. Our everyday consumption leaves a mark, like a footprint in the sand. The land space needed for each economic activity varies. For instance, for transportation, bicycles are the most sustainable, consuming less resources than riding on a bus or in a car.

average ecological footprint is calculated in terms of the total amount of productive land area divided by the human population. The worldwide average ecological footprint is thus 5.4 global acres. It exceeds the 4.4 global acres of productive land and water areas that are available per person on average, while leaving no space for other species. The population of other species keeps plummeting, even though the human population continues to grow.[45] Thus, the ecological deficit has reached 1 acre per person.

Humanity, as a whole, is consuming more resources than can be provided by the earth. The deficit comes, in particular, from North America, which has a higher per capita footprint than any other region on earth.[46] The ecological footprint of the average North American is eight times higher than that of the average African.[47] The ecological footprint per person in the United States is 9.57 hectares (23.65 acres), the highest on the planet.

Since the ecological capacity of the United States is almost half the footprint, the ecological footprint reflects a huge imbalance. In comparison, the ecological footprint of the average German is approximately half that of an average American. The U.S. figures can also be compared with those of Sweden, which has an ecological surplus (its ecological capacity is 18.1 acres; its ecological footprint, 16.6 acres).[48]

Even with gross inequalities in the world, we are exceeding the earth's capacity by 20 percent.[49] The United States faces an 80 percent ecological deficit, which is being borrowed from their grandchildren's generation and from elsewhere in the world. If all the earth inhabitants were to consume as much energy and resources at the level most Americans do, humankind would require a total of three planets.

At the rate of the current population growth and consumption levels, the global ecological footprint continues to surpass the amount of renewable biocapacity on the planet. In its biannual report, World Wildlife Fund International documented that humanity's ecological footprint has breached the limits of the regenerative and absorptive capacity of nature.[50] We are using up more resources than nature can replace or reproduce and are producing far more waste than nature can safely absorb.

The ecological footprint reveals that nature has been utilized beyond its capacity for renewal and regeneration. It is well illustrated by the decline of the world's major marine fisheries and the steady depletion of fossil fuels. Along with the increase in humanity's ecological footprint, terrestrial, freshwater, and marine populations declined by 40 percent between 1970 and 2000.[51]

In the late 1970s, the ecological footprint breached the sustainability mark for the first time and it has continued to increase ever since. Given a twenty-five year growth trend, the global footprint has remained unsustainable beyond renewable biocapacity. Less undeveloped land will be left for future generations if the earth's natural capital continues to be drawn down with nature's absorptive sinks being swamped. In addition, the existence of disparities between income groups reveals stark distributive implications related to environmental equity.

The national footprint is a total area used for industrial and agricultural production, the absorption of energy consumption as well as space for building infrastructure. It is affected by the population size, average consumption per person, and types of production systems.

The regional make-up and size of a footprint reflect the levels of economic income and patterns of consumption. The factors contributing to a national or regional ecological footprint vary in a number of ways. The carbon dioxide emitted from burning fossil fuel typically constitutes the largest portion of the energy component. Carbon dioxide levels in 2002 were 18 percent higher than in 1960 and were estimated to be 31 percent higher since the onset of the Industrial Revolution in 1750. The global use of coal, oil, and natural gas was 4.7 times higher in 2002 than in 1950. The increase in fossil fuel consumption is followed by the utilization of cropland and pasture land.[52] The gross domestic product (GDP) and energy use tend to be highly correlated, since the high level of oil and natural gas consumption is concentrated in wealthy countries.

Since the link between unsustainable consumption and higher income levels is evident, consumption and waste output in rich countries will have to be reduced in order to move toward a sustainable global footprint. In a response to this call, the Netherlands' per capita ecological footprint decreased by 2.5 percent in 2000, with a commitment to control consumption and to protect open spaces, even though the country's footprint is already smaller than the Western European average.

While the responsibility may fall most heavily on wealthier countries, the burden does not rest only with these countries alone. Even if North America and Western Europe succeed in reducing the size of their footprints, the gains can be swamped by an increase in per capita footprint in more populous countries such as China and India. The rising expectations of a growing population result in increasing consumption of scarce resources. The size of global footprints is a function of the levels of human population growth and the concomitant demands on natural resources.

FUTURE STRATEGIES

The reduction of a global footprint requires population stabilization, the utilization of resource-saving technologies, the adoption of policies oriented toward creating less pollution, and the limited use of disposable products. For a sustainable future, the consumption of natural gas and diesel needs to be reduced, along with the exploration of solar and other renewable energy sources as well as increased recycling, reuse, and restrictions on packaging. The improved health of the ecological systems and efficient resource management are essential to expanding bioproductive capacity.

The residents of Jühnde, a village in Lower Saxony of Germany, meet their own energy needs by generating the electricity and heat produced by a biogas plant that is fueled by renewable agricultural products specially grown on 370 acres (150 hectares) of arable land. The renewable raw materials do not emit any carbon dioxide.[53]

Urban dwellers especially with higher levels of consumption have more options to reduce their footprints without reduction in the quality of life. Efforts to help citizens become aware of their own impact on the planet can be part of a broader campaign to improve sustainability. Residents in the municipality of Almada, located near Lisbon, Portugal, are encouraged to consider their quality of life over high consumption by measuring progress toward greater sustainability. The measure has been featured in their city magazine, with an article encouraging individuals to calculate their own ecological footprint.

Cities around the world consume 75 percent of global resources in tandem with the production of a similar percentage of waste. The roads of many cities are choked with pollution and traffic along with overpopulation. One exception is Curitiba, in Brazil, which has been known as one of the most environmentally friendly cities. The city has expanded green space tenfold per person while recycling 70 percent of its waste. A subway system and bicycle lanes were introduced to cut down on traffic pollution.

⑥

Cleaner Consumption
and Production

A visitor from outer space, examining modern industrial economies, might well decide that their main purpose was to turn raw materials into waste. For they produce vast amounts of it—5 tons a year of solid waste for every European, far more for each citizen of the United States of America.

—Klaus Toepfer, Executive Director of the United Nations Environmental Programme, 2003.

The throwaway culture produces unsustainable levels of residues and waste while emissions of carbon dioxide and acidifying gases create environmental burdens. An average person in an advanced industrialized country throws away 100 aluminum drink cans, 70 steel cans, 100 glass bottles or jars, and 100 pounds of plastic every year. A car or computer breaks down and loses its economic value. It is turned into waste, along with its corrosion products and poisonous liquids. Newspaper turns into waste after being read. Even though it is made of wood, an organic material, it will take years for the newspapers to be transformed into topsoil.

The millions of other species on our planet produce useful by-products, but the residuals of human production and consumption generate worthless waste. Nature provides services to assimilate human waste as well as supplying humans with both raw materials and products. Industrial civilization thrives on materials mined from enriched deposits such as ores and fossil fuels. Industrial waste is different in composition from the product of the biosphere and cannot be decomposed in natural systems. Metallurgical activities, such as producing, using, and discarding industrial goods, increase the chemical composition of air, water, and soil, along with a surge in CO^2 concentrations in the atmosphere.

ECO-EFFICIENCY

The efficiency of material use needs to be improved along the life cycle of a product. The best way to prevent waste is to change the way goods are produced at the front end of the material cycles.[54] By reducing the material intensity of production, eco-efficiency can help a producer achieve economically competitive advantage.

Resource productivity measures the degree of efficiency of natural material input into the economy. The efficiency can be measured by dividing the gross domestic product (GDP) with direct material input composed of both domestic and imported natural resources. Eco-efficiency can be improved by reducing the input of raw material and expanding the reuse of resources. The higher ratio of reused and recycled resources to total material input in a production process is desirable.

Efficiency in the use of primary materials extracted from nature, both at home and abroad, is significantly different among various countries. The United States uses approximately more than 90 tons per capita, while the European Union uses about 50 tons per capita. The increase in per capita total material input indicates continuous pressure on the global environment, resulting from the extraction of energy, metals, and mineral resources.

The level of resource extraction indicates, in a general way, the "hidden flows" of mining wastes and emissions. The flow of production input can be examined in terms of the different potential for pollution and ill health posed by specific chemicals or materials.

In March 2003, the Japanese government passed a resolution on the Basic Plan for Establishing a Recycling-Based
Society. The national program (with the goal of reducing total
waste in half, from approximately 56 million tons for 2000 to
approximately 28 million tons for 2010) was designed to initiate
a shift towards sustainable patterns of production and consumption by curbing the use of natural resources as much
as possible. The target for a final disposal amount was set in
light of a shortage of landfill sites in Japan. To achieve these
targets, laws and regulations were developed for waste management and recycling.[55]

Cleaner production and eco-efficiency can be achieved by
generating as little waste as possible along with the utilization
of what has already been produced. Only the rich 20 percent of
the world population are in a privileged position to consume
and waste. In low-income countries, the main components
of municipal solid waste are readily used again without legisla-
tion.[56] The earth can support a maximum of 10 billion people
even with zero waste.[57]

Everything has a place before, during and after use. The value
of labor and raw material such as metal is still embedded in the
commodity after it is discarded.[58] Raw materials and energy can
be recovered from waste, including metals from scrap and heat
from combustibles.[59] The components of many products are still
considered resources even after their use. Roof tiles are made
from spent cans, fuel briquettes from cardboard, and packing
material from newspapers.

Parts of products can be used for different applications.
We can reduce waste generation and lessen waste disposal by
saving lumber and other building materials after demoli-
tions. Furniture, appliances, tools, electronics, and copiers can
be repaired or remanufactured. One way to respond to an
intractable waste problem of car tires is to retread and use them
again (Figure 6.1). Some of the hundreds of millions of used
car tires collected worldwide each year have also been converted

Figure 6.1 Expanding markets for the reuse of scrap tires have enabled the state of Ohio to reduce its tire stockpiles more quickly. Workers at this site plan to shred around ten million tires over the next 30 months. Another way to respond to the burgeoning waste problem of used tires is to retread them and use them again.

into artificial reefs that protect land from erosion by the sea. In addition, the controlled burning of tires can produce good quality fuel, given their clean burning and higher heating value than coal.

Recycled paper is used to make newspapers, cardboard, cereal boxes, and wrapping paper. Recycled plastic is useful for tables, benches, bicycle racks, cameras, backpacks, clothes, shoes, and soda bottles. Iron and steel can be used as raw materials for the manufacture of cars, bicycles, refrigerators, and machines. Rubber can be remolded to make playground equipment, speed bumps, and bulletin boards. Green buildings can rely on renewable energy such as wind and solar power and the use of water-conserving toilets.

In order to encourage recycling, disposal funds would be used to collect and process resources. Instead of subsidizing industries that allow waste of raw materials and pollution of air and water, a zero-waste society would give tax breaks to companies that use recycled materials. The manufacturers and consumers would be encouraged to recycle the product at its end use.[60]

In Germany, all manufacturers and distributors are obliged to take back and recycle sales packaging. A large share of textiles are reused (40 percent) or recycled (50 percent). Industries established voluntary commitments for the recycling of old car parts (95 percent until 2015).[61]

All waste paper, cardboard, wood, plastic bottles, metal containers, and broken appliances can be used again as raw material for production instead of being piled up in landfills. The sustainable management of waste can be achieved by reduction in the negative impact of consumption through recycling.

METHODS OF DISPOSAL

The two most common methods of waste disposal are landfill and incineration. Trash can be burned in an incinerator, a device similar to a furnace. While incinerators can quickly eliminate the bulk of trash, serious risks are posed by pollution from incineration plants. Harmful chemicals from smoke and ash left over from burning trash can cause harm to humans as well as other animal and plant life.

The most common means of disposal are landfills, huge holds with a layer of clay or plastic in the ground where much of our garbage gets dumped. It takes a long time for trash to rot away in landfills (Figure 6.2). Landfills are used for compacting and burying our garbage in low-lying areas. Improperly designed landfills fail to keep dangerous liquids from seeping into the groundwater supply. If disposal treatment is not carried out to the highest standards, the soil is polluted with heavy metals, persistent organic chemicals, and other poisons.[62] In addition,

Figure 6.2   The most common means of disposal are landfills. One day's municipal waste in the United States weighs more that 100 million tons.

rotting garbage in landfills emits methane, which contributes to global warming.

One day's municipal waste in the United States weighs more than 100 million tons, an amount that would fill 50,000 garbage trucks. More than half of U.S. municipalities experience landfill shortages. Because of their unhealthful and unsightly materials, landfills are not welcomed by most communities.

Paper, paper products, and organic material (for example, food scraps, leftovers, and yard waste) constitute 60 to 70 percent of all domestic waste by weight. As the largest single component of municipal solid waste, the share of paper and paper products in the total of domestic waste has grown above 35 percent since 2000. Glass, in the form of bottles, jars, light bulbs, windows, and cups, constitutes about 6 to 8 percent of a landfill's waste. About 9 percent is composed of metals (for example, aluminum and food cans). Approximately 2 to 5 percent of the municipal waste comes from textiles, clothes, and fabrics made from natural fibers and sources such as wool, cotton, leathers, and rubber. Chemicals in batteries, tablets, pills, paints, solvents, medicines account for 3 percent. These toxic chemicals can pollute the ground or water. Electronic trash made up of old or broken computers, cellular phones, video games, TVs, and radios also includes toxic substances like lead, mercury, and cadmium.

Plastics are the fastest growing proportion of municipal total waste because manufacturers find it easy to shape plastic to package their products. Plastics, including plastic bags, containers, and bottles, constituted only 0.4 percent of the total municipal solid waste in 1960, but increased to 10.7 percent by 2000. Plastics are not biodegradable and therefore do not break down through organic processes.

Much of paper, cloth, glass, plastic, metals, wood, rubber, leather, and textiles can be recycled. Most food scraps can be used to make compost for gardens and green spaces, keeping the soil healthy. High proportions of organic compounds (vegetable peelings, debris and other food scraps, leftovers, yard waste, untreated wood and sheetrock) are biodegradable and can be transferred to a composting facility.

TRANSFER OF WASTE

Given their threat to human health and the environment, hazardous waste from industrial processes and products is a worldwide challenge. With more stringent environmental protection regulations and higher disposal costs in their own countries, rich countries often sought an alternative solution to waste disposal by dumping toxic materials on poor countries. Eventually international agreements were reached to control the transboundary movement of hazardous waste, that is, the movement of hazardous wastes across international frontiers. In 1989, a measure adopted under the Basel Convention banned toxic waste exports from highly industrialized countries to less developed ones, with the goal of protecting human health and the environment against the ill effects of hazardous wastes.[63]

The legal framework was further strengthened later by the adoption of a protocol on liability and compensation for damage resulting from the movement of industrial waste and its disposal. In particular, the agreement prevents any shipment intended for disposal in Antarctica. Global bans are also imposed on dumping industrial and radioactive waste in the oceans, two-thirds of the earth's surface.

These decisions do more than just stop direct pollution. They are also a driving force, providing an incentive for industries to employ clean production methods, thus minimizing the production of hazardous waste in the first place. Thus, the Basel Convention is not just about prohibiting pollution being transferred from richer to poorer countries, but rather it is one of the most important instruments in promoting a clean production-based economy that is a prerequisite for sustainable development.

ENVIRONMENTAL RISKS TO HUMAN HEALTH

Contamination of the air, soil, and water with hazardous waste causes health risks. Air, soil, and water pollution, conditions called "environmental risks," remain the primary source of ill health for the world population. The main causes of environmental threats to health include a lack of safe water and sanitation, indoor and outdoor air pollution, and natural resource degradation.

Every year 15 million people are killed due to chemical contamination and waterborne diseases. The source of this pollution is agricultural and industrial waste, which is choking our rivers and poisoning our groundwater.[64] Contaminated water may come from the unsafe use of chemicals as well as inadequate solid and hazardous waste management. Poor sanitation, indoor smoke, deficient food hygiene, and unsafe waste disposal are usually associated with factors such as poverty and social exclusion, the barriers to participation in society.

The production and use of industrial toxic chemicals, which was virtually unknown before the 19th century, now pose a major threat to humankind and the environment. The increased pollution from synthetic chemicals is ascribed to rapid industrialization, urbanization, and intensified agriculture.[65] Each year 2.5 million metric tons of herbicides, fungicides, and insecticides are released in ecosystems.[66]

Toxic substances released into the air, food, or water originate from the emissions of cars, industrial processes, and waste treatment processes such as incinerators. Toxic substances are also produced by the excessive use of pesticides such as DDT and fertilizers for agricultural and domestic purposes. Toxic heavy metals (including lead, mercury, nickel, cadmium, and chromium) and pollutants (including dioxins and polychlorinated biphenyls) are of particular concern, since they do not readily degrade in the environment and accumulate in plants, fish, shellfish, animals, and humans. These substances can travel long distances and can easily move up the food chain.

Since their introduction in the early 1960s, synthetic pesticides have been polluting rivers, groundwater, air, soil, and food. The elements of pesticides penetrate the human body through eating, drinking, and breathing, and interfere with the regulation of biological growth. Infants are particularly at risk, since DDT can damage the body's ability to fend off diseases.

Marine Pollution

Many people in the world live near the coast, where the human impact on the water is most keenly felt. Over three-quarters of all the seas' pollutants come from land-based human activities, such as the direct dumping of sewage and toxic waste into the sea. Biological systems have been disturbed by the discharge of phosphates, nitrates, organic chemicals, and many other substances into the seas.[67]

Persistent organic pollutants contaminate the oceans and the air distant from manufacturing sites, threatening the health of even remote polar regions. The contamination of the marine environment and polar regions can be brought under control only by a complete ban on producing and using organochlorines and other chemicals throughout the world.

Health Impact of Water Pollution

The scarcity and misuse of fresh water pose a serious threat to human health, welfare, food security, and the entire ecosystem. In developing countries, the lack of water often forces people to depend on unsafe sources. While polluted water can cause a range of serious infections, diseases can also arise from an insufficient water supply that does not permit regular hand washing.

Biological contaminants and chemical pollutants as well as atmospheric pollution compromise water quality, as do agricultural waste and deforestation. Contaminated water is responsible for a third of all deaths and 80 percent of all disease in developing countries. Polluted water affects the health of 1.2 billion people worldwide. Every year 4 billion cases of diarrhea are reported, and 6 million people become blind from trachoma.[68]

Diarrhea kills about 2.2 million people a year, equivalent to 20 jumbo jets crashing every day.[69] The dramatic rise in cholera cases is attributed to deteriorating water systems and malnutrition. Contaminated water is blamed for a range of potentially life-threatening diseases, such as cholera, typhoid, and viral hepatitis.[70]

Biological contaminants of water sources include parasites, bacteria, and viruses. They enter the drinking water supply when the water source is polluted by human or animal waste and sewage. The most important source of water contamination in developing countries is the lack of adequate sanitation facilities. Today, about 2.4 billion people do not have access to even a simple lavatory.[71]

Low capacity in the treatment of wastewater is a major factor causing water pollution in most parts of the developing world. In Latin America, only about 14 percent of urban wastewater receives proper treatment before discharge. Although the level of sewage treatment is reported to be higher among Asian cities (on average about 35 percent), it is still unacceptable, since most of wasted water is directly drained to seas, lakes, and rivers.[72] Poor water management strategies, combined with habitat modifications (such as land conversion and forest clearance for roads and agriculture), also give rise to water quality degradation, consequently increasing vector-borne disease transmissions.

Specific Health Threats To Children

The range of environmental effects in health is diverse, often unpredictable in magnitude, and sometimes slow to emerge. Sadly, children are especially susceptible to the threats of environmental hazards. Because of their smaller physical size, immature organs, and insufficient knowledge, children are particularly vulnerable to environmental threats. Prior to being born, infants face environmental harm in their mother's womb. Children who embody our dreams also inherit our legacies, such as the consequences of our mistreatment of nature.

The yearly death of nearly 11 million children is related to readily preventable causes. Biological contaminants cause a series of deadly childhood illnesses in developing countries. Human waste heavily pollutes many rivers and lakes in developing countries. Diarrhea diseases along with malaria constitute the biggest cause of childhood mortality.

The availability and quality of water as well as its proper management determine a child's well being. Unsanitary conditions and practices at the household level, such as absence of sanitary lavatories, unsafe waste disposal, and unhygienic behavior in childcare and food preparation, create a dangerous environment with health risks to children.[73]

Sustainable Development

Only when the last tree has died and the last river been poisoned and the last fish has been caught will we realize that we cannot eat money.

—A 19th-Century Proverb of Cree Indian Origin

The earth's ecosystems affect our well being directly through supplying food, water, timber, genetic resources, and raw materials for industrial production. They have an impact on poverty, health, livelihoods, security, and economic development by providing such services as flood control, soil regeneration, pollination, maintenance of air quality, and the provision of aesthetic and cultural benefits.

With the decreasing amount of oceanic fisheries, grasslands, forests and croplands, renewable resource bases are shrinking. Acid rain caused by air pollution devastates crops and forests. Human activities such as intensive agricultural production exceed the capacity of the land for its renewal. Local environmental degradation derived from soil erosion and desertification is especially severe in developing countries.

Oil and coal have been supplemented by the use of nuclear energy. However, nuclear accidents at Three Mile Island in the U.S. (1979) and at Chernobyl in the former Soviet Union (1986) demonstrated the possibility of a catastrophic nuclear accident (Figure 7.1). On the other hand, development of renewable natural energy sources has shown to be a very time-consuming process.

According to the 1987 report of the World Commission on Environment and Development (WCED), entitled "Our Common Future," the strategy for sustainable development should be oriented toward meeting the material aspirations of the present generation without compromising the ability of future generations. "The health of our planet and its people is the most important legacy that we will leave for future generations."[74] Economic growth in the present should not sacrifice the living conditions of future generations by undermining their ability to live secure, productive, and fulfilling lives.

Unsustainable economic growth diminishes the earth's long-term capacity to support life. Sustainable development is necessary to deal with the causes of global climate change, acid rain, and air pollution. At the same time, it is important to recognize that worsening environmental conditions deepen poverty and inequality. Sharing and managing natural resources is critical for the future survival of various communities.

Projected demographic changes and economic growth will lead to an increasing demand for biological resources. This implies an even greater impact on ecosystems and their resources needed to provide goods and services. In many instances, the primary sources of environmental misuse are related to commercial interests and thoughtless government policies. For example, logging may provide export income, but it destroys the land available for food production and water supply.

Responding to our planet's eroding capacity to sustain us is the greatest challenge facing the human race at the dawn of

Figure 7.1   The reactor at Unit 2 of the Three Mile Island Nuclear Facility ceased operations after a partial meltdown on March 28, 1979. This was the most serious nuclear reactor accident in U.S. history. It took 12 years and $1 billion for the reactor to be repaired and reopened. The reactor involved in the accident was destroyed and Unit 1 went back into service. The seriousness of this situation raised public awareness and apprehension about the risks of nuclear power.

the 21st century. Addressing the depletion of resources, poverty, and economic disparity has become an important global agenda for sustainable development. The types and levels of production and consumption of goods on a global level must be brought into line with the finite ability of the earth to sustain them.

POVERTY AND ITS ENVIRONMENTAL IMPACT

Our fate on this small planet is inextricably linked. One-fourth of the world remains in a desperate poverty trap, and millions lose the struggle for survival every year. Overcoming this chaotic struggle for life means the ability and opportunity of people to obtain access to sustainable daily necessities.

It is the poor, especially women and children, who suffer the most from the deterioration of major ecosystems. In many low-income countries, women have to spend a considerable amount of their day looking for wood so that they can cook. Children are often sick due to lack of access to safe drinking water and to heavy pollution.[75] Poverty, widespread in the developing world, contributes to the deterioration of natural resources as well as being an underlying cause of both ill-health and under-nourishment. In today's $30-trillion global economy, 2.8 billion people survive on less than $2 a day; 1.2 billion people struggle to meet their basic needs with less than $1 per day and more than half of them are children.[76]

Resource degradation and pollution result from careless and excessive consumption and ineffective resource use. Those inhabiting ecologically vulnerable areas are severely affected by other people's wasteful habits. Almost all waste dumps are located in major urban areas, creating hazardous living conditions, including unpleasant smells and an unsightly view.

Two billion people worldwide have to burn wood, charcoal, dung, and other forms of low-quality fuels, usually on open stoves and fires, to meet cooking and heating needs.[77] A mix of poisonous chemicals included in the smoke is often the cause of acute asthma, respiratory infections, and cancer. Poor people drain their fragile natural resource bases with deforestation and wildlife trade as well as unsustainable fishing and agriculture. Many countries have stripped their resources bare to earn foreign currency that is needed to buy such basic necessities as food and fuel.

LIMITS OF CONVENTIONAL ECONOMIC GROWTH

The well-being of a society cannot be measured only by such criteria as national earnings or gross domestic product without consideration of their proper linkages to environmental health and social well-being.[78] A wide array of marine life, forests, and other natural capital is essential to addressing the question of how to sustain contemporary patterns of development. On the other hand, various forms of ecosystem services (such as preserving and regenerating soil, recycling nutrients, pollinating crops, controlling floods, and fixing nitrogen and carbon) often go unrecorded in economic transactions.

A myriad of nature's services are missed or typically underpriced because they usually do not come with a price tag. National accounts miss changes brought about by economic activities to the stocks of many natural resources. The value of natural capital is often impossible to esablish because it is often mobile (birds, butterflies, river water, and the atmosphere). Ensuring environmental sustainability should be considered as one of the main components of development strategies along with the efforts to reduce poverty. More poverty is produced with the accumulation of wealth, which can lead to damaging the environment.

THE CONCEPT OF SUSTAINABLE DEVELOPMENT

Sustainable development was thrust into the mainstream of world debate as one of the possible ways to tackle environmental deterioration derived from reckless economic activities. In particular, the debate is centered on the following two questions. First, is it possible to increase the basic standard of living of the world's expanding population without unnecessarily depleting the earth's finite natural resources and degrading the environment upon which we all depend? Second, can humanity collectively step back from the brink of environmental collapse and at the same time lift its poorest members up to the level of basic human health and dignity enjoyed by many in economically advanced countries?

Development needs to be balanced with the sustainability of ecological goods and services. Even though converting a forest to agriculture may increase crop production, it may also decrease the supply of clean water, flood control, and biodiversity. When shrimp farms are created, mangrove swamps are destroyed, thus causing a reduction in commercial fish species along with migratory birds, sea turtles, manatees, and dolphins. An integrated framework for the use of land, coasts, and oceans needs to be geared toward sustainable management and conservation.

Sustainable development is therefore ultimately about reestablishing our relationships with each other and with the planet on which we live by countering the negative impact of unsustainable production and consumption patterns on poverty and the environment. Meeting local environmental and livelihood needs can be compatible with global environmental sustainability. Some examples of how this can be done include the sustainable use of forest products for the generation of alternative sources of income; the use of agricultural wastes in biogas production as an alternative to fuel wood from forests; and integrated insect control for improved food production.

GREEN LABELING

Increased consumer awareness and choice can promote innovative environmental policies. The term green labeling refers to labeling that conveys information about the environmental impact of producing, processing, transporting, or using a natural product. Companies are encouraged to use green labeling to promote sustainable business practice by increasing consumer awareness.

Sustainable wood is grown on plantations to protect the rich ecosystems of rain forests that are the traditional sources of wood. Newly planted trees replace old ones that were cut down for continued supply. However, the persistent international demand for cheap timber, along with people's ignorance and indifference to the origin of wood products, drives irresponsible cutting of tropical forests.

Green labeling educates consumers not to buy products made from tropical plants and animals. More land has been carved out from the rain forest after the soil was ruined due to several years of intensive grazing. Some consumers have chosen not to buy the meat of cattle raised on ranches following the destruction of tropical forests.

As part of the efforts to set standards for sustainable forestry, the independent Forest Stewardship Council (FSC) was established with support of the World Wildlife Fund (WWF), an organization known for its dedication to international conservation. FSC principles and criteria are applied to accrediting corporations that are able to prove healthy management of forests. A certificate is granted to logging companies which cause as little damage as possible to the forests. Sustainable supplies are permitted to bear the FSC's label for the purpose of guiding buyers to purchase timber and wood products from well-managed forests.[79]

The sustainable forestry certificate helped some cities and stores boycott tropical wood (including mahogany, teak, and rosewood) often made into boats, furniture, doors, and musical instruments. The timber from tropic rain forests is also used to make outdoor furniture, since it has a good reputation for resisting decay. More forest is cleared to keep up the supply every time people purchase products made from rainforest wood. Logging companies will not cut trees in the rain forests if people do not purchase the lumber.

The long-term sustainability of the marine ecosystem has been under serious threat with the increasing demand and depleting supply of global fish stocks. For example, some 27 million tons of captured fish are abandoned annually after being caught; shrimp fishing is the most wasteful since it amounts to one-third of the total discarded fish.

The Marine Stewardship Council (MSC) was created to address the fishing crisis. It has the support by over 100 major seafood processors, traders, and retailers. MSC runs a certification scheme for sustainable fisheries. The MSC adopted principles and criteria that are closely based on the Code of Responsible Fisheries created by the Food and Agriculture Organization (FAO) of the UN.

As an accrediting professional body, the MSC has been assessing and certifying fisheries around the world since early 1999. More than 100 certified fisheries bear the MSC logo on their packaging, so that consumers can choose products from well-managed fisheries. The certified fish products have been caught in a way that preserves supplies for the future. In this way, the market will help encourage responsible fishing. The MSC's future success depends on consumer awareness and recognition of its logo.

RENEWABLE ENERGY

Approximately four-fifths of the world's primary energy supply comes from fossil fuels (about one-half from oil, one-third from coal, and the remainder from natural gas). They are mostly consumed by industrially advanced countries with less than a fifth of humanity. In particular, per capita emissions in North America are ten times as much as in all the developing countries combined.

The release of gases from the combustion of coal, oil, and natural gas are the most serious contributors to pollution and global climate changes. Thus, the energy use of the wealthy countries is mainly to blame for the emission of most carbon dioxide and the resultant global warming. In addition, fossil fuel is unsustainable, since it cannot be reused and is eventually depleted.

The gross disparity in per capita energy use is reflected by the fact that in the least developed countries, electricity use per capita is only 1 percent of what it is in the industrialized nations. In some countries traditional biomass, such as wood and dung, provide over 90 percent of national energy supplies.[80] If energy had to be apportioned evenly, only one-sixth of the current energy use would be available to people living in North America.

The consumption of fossil fuels in both industrialized and developing countries can be reduced through energy efficiency measures with expanded use of renewable energy sources. While energy generated by hydroelectric power from big dams flood land and wildlife habitats, such forms of renewable sources of energy as solar and wind energy could do much to improve energy efficiency, since they are self-renewing resources.[81] Only a tiny fraction of this energy is harnessed for human needs, mainly because it has not been explored sufficiently. Expensive fuel imports can be cut back, while making renewable forms of energy much more widely available to poor people.

Even though access to clean energy would not be adequate enough to ensure sustainable development, it is a vital part of our strategies to alleviate poverty.[82] The adoption of advanced renewable technologies reduces the dependence on imported oil and permits the devotion of scarce foreign exchange earnings to critical social investments in education, health, and other welfare sectors. Measures that increase the efficiency of energy use with the promotion of renewable energy can serve as a tool to reach multiple development objectives, including improved food production and cleaner water supplies. More than 1 million households in the developing world are run by solar energy, with wind capacity powering more than 5 million typical homes.[83]

Renewable energy is ecologically as well as economically beneficial. Clean sources of energy—the sun, wind, thermal, tidal, and wave power—can help tackle a lack of supply of electricity and decrease pollution (Figure 7.2). Less than 5 percent of energy consumption is covered by electricity derived from wind, solar, geothermal, biomass, and small hydropower technologies. With the expansion of the renewable energy industry to be worth over $10 billion per year, however, 30 major firms plan to invest from $10 to $15 billion in the next five years.

The full utilization of the solar energy received on earth in a single day would support human activities for more than 15 years. Distributed free by nature and without danger of depletion, energy directly from sunlight can bring electricity to the

Figure 7.2   These solar panels at a power plant at Carrizo Plains, California, are one type of renewable energy that is ecologically as well as economically beneficial, but today less than 5 percent of energy consumption is derived from the sun or wind, or geothermal, biomass, and hydropower sources.

scattered villages where about half the world's people live. While solar energy is an inexhaustible fuel with low maintenance costs, its environmental impact is minimal. For example, unlike current forms of electricity, solar energy can be installed directly in most residential homes, reducing the need for transmission and distribution facilities.

The Netherlands aims to have 100,000 homes fitted with solar panels by the year 2010. India has favorable commercial financing and complementary regulations that will support the expansion of solar energy, wind farms, and mini-hydro stations. Sri Lanka's Energy Services Delivery Project introduced solar electricity to almost 20,000 Sri Lankan homes with the aid of innovative micro-financing programs. Solar energy has also been used to provide electricity and hot water in Peru, Ghana, and China. Solar hot water heaters have been installed in homes and businesses with less cost than conventional water heating in Morocco.

Turbines can be driven by steam from hot rocks (geothermal heat kept in the interior of the earth) to produce pollution-free power. They can be used in places where natural heat is found not far below the surface. Geothermal energy arises from heat trapped inside the earth, about 30 miles below the surface. Nearly 3,000 megawatts of capacity (enough to support over 3 million people) are produced at sites for electric power generation currently operating in California, Nevada, Hawaii, and Utah.[84]

Biomass, which includes wood by-products and agricultural wastes, generates electricity and produces heat and liquid fuels for transportation. Wood chips, switchgrass, and solid waste are burned in a power plant in Burlington, Vermont, to produce a substance similar to natural gas. Whereas the oldest use of biomass energy is simply burning wood and straw, technical advances in the science of bioenergy have allowed the conversion of agricultural wastes and organic material into fuels and other products. Experiments have shown that agricultural waste can be transformed from a problem to a valuable resource, producing electricity, cooking gas, and heat that can foster rural development.

By growing one's own fuel, bioenergy's potential benefit is huge both economically and environmentally. New conversion technologies increased the income of farmers by turning corn stalks and wheat straw into ethanol after the cash crop was sold. A wide variety of agricultural "waste" is converted to produce chemicals and plastics currently made from fossil fuels as well as providing fuel for the transportation sector.

Most ethanol is produced from corn, using only the starch in the kernels. Currently ethanol and other renewable resources account for 3.4 per cent of U.S. gas consumption.[85] Ethanol burns cleanly, creating little smoke. Thus ethanol offers multiple benefits from aiding farmers to enhancing the nation's energy security. With gasoline prices reaching all-time highs and the threat of climate change to the stability of the world's ecosystem, development of clean, abundant biofuels such as ethanol should be a priority.

The expansion of the market for energy-efficient products accelerates the worldwide transition to clean energy. Energy-efficient lights, heating, and cooling devices can bring about financial and commercial benefits, including savings of large amounts of electricity. In Poland, sales of over 1.2 million of compact fluorescent lamps in three years resulted from lower prices (through a manufacturer subsidy) combined with a mass media campaign.

WATER CONSERVATION

In terms of our water supply, vast savings are possible through conservation. Modern toilets consume at least 1.5 gallons of water for each flush. (Keep in mind that is the same amount of daily water use for people in many developing countries.) There is an incredible amount of waste that accompanies water usage. Even in the industrialized societies such as the Great Britain, a quarter of the water is wasted due to leaky pipes. Irrigating fields leads to the evaporation or trickling away of 20 to 30 percent of the water used. The paper industry alone generates about 1,551 billion gallons of wastewater each year.[86]

Water usage can be reduced by recycling municipal and industrial wastewater combined with increased efficiency of water use in agriculture. The cheapest means of improving water supply is to minimize the waste of water for industrial production, irrigation, bathing, and lavatory flushing. Local communities and industries need to channel wastewater back into the ground to recharge supplies. Conserving water must play an important part in reducing the proportion of people without ready access to drinking water and sanitation by half in the next ten years. Consumer education as well as reduced water subsidies is necessary to enhance the awareness of water conservation and even encourage people away from a meat-rich, water-intensive diet.

Recycling wastewater is also an effective means for agriculture, which has the biggest consumption of water. Treated wastewater is increasingly used to grow fruit and vegetables in California, and provides 30 percent of the farm water supply in Israel. In addition, drip irrigation that delivers water directly to plants' roots and low-pressure sprinklers that avoid over-watering to reduce water usage. Drip irrigation has decreased water use by 30 to 70 percent in California, Spain, India, Israel, and Jordan, even as it increases crop yields.[87]

In less industrialized countries, the use of water is concentrated on agriculture. Newly designed low-cost drip and sprinkler systems can be introduced to many poor rural communities, as is illustrated by the use of a $5 bucket sprinkler kit needed to water vegetable plots in a northern Himalayan village. The use of simple, low-cost irrigation and water storage technologies has become a main concern across Africa.

Industrial recycling systems are designed to catch wastewater and use it again in operations for production of steel and other primary metals, electronics, paper, chemicals, and petroleum, processes that consume a lot of water. In-house recycling and waste treatment systems have reduced operational costs. Xerox invested $50,000 in conservation equipment at one of its facilities and saved $38,000 in the first year alone. In particular, the savings have proved substantial for a semiconductor manufacturer that has heavy water dependency.[88]

Tighter regulations governing water-using appliances can be introduced in industrialized countries, where households consume vast quantities of water in washing, lavatory flushing, and gardening. Government regulations have required sales of low-flow lavatories in the United States. Reduction in water use has been achieved by the replacement of 350,000 old lavatories with low-flush ones in Mexico City.

Underpriced water is responsible for overuse; rising usage fees will help ensure less waste of water. Water can be priced to penalize excessive users and reward conservers. In some countries, tiered pricing systems have been adopted to discourage overuse. In South Africa, increasing fees are imposed on extra use after the supply of 6,000 liters of free water a month.

Global Environmental Agreements

Concerted international responses are essential to fight against global warming and the depletion of the ozone layer, environmental threats that have an impact on everyone on the planet. Other important international efforts include the protection of endangered species and maintenance of biodiversity. Building consensus on the nature of global action is necessary to resolve environmental issues. International agreements can be reached to provide a common framework of action.

BUILDING GLOBAL CONSENSUS ON SUSTAINABLE DEVELOPMENT
The first global conference on environmental issues was held in Stockholm in 1972. There the Conference on Human Environment placed the concept of sustainable development on the world's agenda.

Twenty years later, more specific action plans were adopted at the United Nations World Conference on Environment and Development (UNCED) held in Rio de Janeiro, Brazil. In the years preceding the conference, a series of scientific findings and assessments underlined the dangers of ozone depletion, climate change, and severe threats to important ecosystems.

The Rio summit led to the adoption of Agenda 21, a blueprint for action to achieve sustainable development world-wide.[89] As a roadmap for the new millennium, Agenda 21 stressed the growing international consensus that sustainable development is not an option but a requirement increasingly imposed by the limits of nature. Its 40-chapter program of action covers many aspects of environmental conservation and sustainable development, from health to clean water, oceans, poverty, technology transfer, and waste disposal. In particular, the comprehensive action plan focused on reducing the negative environmental impact of industrialized countries, eliminating poverty worldwide, and stabilizing the level of the human population.

To provide effective follow-up and monitor and report on the implementation of the agreements at the local, national, regional and international levels, the Commission on Sustainable Development was created in December 1992. By using Agenda 21 as the guiding document for government management of ecological systems in most regions of the world, environmental ministers continue to check progress at the annual meeting at the UN Commission for Sustainable Development. Despite the gravity and urgency of the environmental challenges facing the international community, not every country has been enthusiastic about integrating the ideas of sustainable development in government planning, or have delayed their contribution to fulfilling the commitments of Agenda 21. It is one thing for countries to embrace the global environmental principles and quite another to act on them.

Since the first global environmental conference was held in Stockholm, the nature of international cooperation has changed. Along with the creation of new international institutions, multilateral agreements have been developed in areas ranging from a reduction in global warming to the preservation of endangered species. Less developed countries need both financial and technical aid to implement various measures proposed in international agreements. For instance, industrialized countries have been asked to help reduce the foreign debts of developing countries so that they can preserve their resources.

PROTECTION OF THE OZONE LAYER

In the areas of protection of the ozone layer, international negotiations led to the conclusion of Vienna Convention for the Protection of the Ozone Layer that was signed by 21 countries in March 1985. The agreement spells out the obligation of countries to control activities that may adversely affect the ozone layer. Most importantly, participating states pledged cooperation to reduce the production and emissions of chlorofluorocarbons (CFCs). The Vienna Convention also provided fact-finding and non-compulsory dispute settlement systems to handle the problem of noncompliance.

The Montreal Protocol on Substances that Deplete the Ozone Layer, signed by twenty-seven countries in September 1987, provided plans for a gradual phase-out of trade of ozone-depleting chemicals with measures to control their consumption. The provisions included collecting data on production and consumption of CFCs, sharing technical information, and promoting technical assistance needed to comply with the protocol.

Wealthy countries accepted their responsibility and agreed to take the lead by using a variety of taxes, rules, and education programs as well as research on substitutes for CFCs. The financial and technology transfer provisions specify that a fund would be created to pay the costs for developing countries to meet their control obligations by switching to substitutes. Sanctions are supposed to be employed against noncompliance with trade restrictions on controlled substances and their products.

Through another round of international negotiations concluded in London (June 1990), participating states accepted the mandate of phasing out all major ozone-depleting substances. Along with the commitment laid out in the agreement, the production of the most damaging ozone-depleting substances was eliminated in developed countries (except for a few critical uses) and should be phased out by 2010 in developing countries. These measures would help the CFC concentration in the ozone layer recover to pre-1980 levels by the year 2050.

REDUCTION IN GLOBAL WARMING

Compared with the efforts to protect the ozone layer, it has proved more difficult to produce agreements that specify a target and timetable for controlling emissions of greenhouse gases. Since emissions from the burning of fossil fuels have been much higher in industrialized countries, these countries have been called on to take a major responsibility. In recent years, dramatic increases in carbon dioxide production in rapidly industrializing countries have also become a serious problem, especially since those countries refuse to take any responsible actions. Thus, while China and India account for more than 20 percent of global emissions, they have opposed the implementation of tougher regulations.

Given the vested interests of powerful corporate groups, the United States has also obstructed key international efforts to establish strong rules and regulations, such as mandated reductions of carbon dioxide. Therefore, the European Community has assumed a lead role in the negotiations. Strong support for negotiation on reduction in the emissions of greenhouse gases has also been demonstrated by small island states that are concerned about rising sea levels.

Scientific consensus following a series of conferences on the atmosphere and climate led to the negotiation of the 1992 Framework Convention on Climate Change signed by 154 countries at the Rio summit. Its objective, as stated in Article 2 of the document, is the stabilization of atmospheric concentrations of greenhouse gases "at a level that would prevent dangerous anthropogenic [derived from human activities] interference with the climate system."

The Convention notes that given their dominant level of emission and wealth, industrialized countries are primarily responsible for addressing climate change at present and have been called upon to take responsibility for mitigating climate change. The provision of financial resources and transfer of technology were promised to meet the full costs incurred from the implementation of the agreement by developing countries. Most industrialized countries broadly pledged to cut down their greenhouse gas emissions to 1990 levels by the year 2000.

While the Convention mentions the restoration of greenhouse gas emissions to earlier levels, it primarily contains pledges to control greenhouse gases, without any legally binding commitment. The Convention's action requirements specified in Article 4 were limited to preparing contingency plans in reducing the level of climate change as well as developing national inventories of anthropogenic emissions.

Eventually legally binding targets and time tables were set in the Kyoto Protocol, an agreement adopted at the Third Climate Conference held in Kyoto, Japan, in December 1997. In the agreement, industrialized countries agreed to a 5.2 percent global cut in the emission of six greenhouse gases. In order to come into force, the Protocol has to be ratified by 55 states whose combined emission aggregate amounts to 55 percent of the world total at 1990 levels.[90]

Overall, the negotiations on climate change have been dominated more by political and economic interests than environmental imperatives. This has been clearly revealed by the Bush administration's consistent opposition to any legally binding agreement such as the Kyoto Protocol. Other roadblocks to action plans for greenhouse gas reduction include formidable technological challenges and steep divisions over the appropriation of the cost.

CONSERVATION OF WILDLIFE AND BIODIVERSITY

Balance between the species, preserved over the last 75 million years, has been seriously threatened by the unprecedented decimation of prime habitat in much of the earth's tropical forests and wetlands. Special protection for the habitats of rare or endangered species, declared in the 1982 UN World Charter for Nature, has drawn growing international attention. The Biodiversity Convention, signed by 157 states at the end of the United Nations Conference on Environment and Development in June 1992, takes a comprehensive approach to conservation efforts through the protection of not only the animal and plant species, but also the maintenance of the habitat where they live.[91]

Other conventions shed light on the preservation of limited categories of wildlife through specific methods such as trade sanctions. The Convention on International Trade in Endangered Species of Wild Fauna and Flora (CITES) controls, reduces, or prohibits the international trade of endangered animals and plant species and their products. The convention came into force in 1973 with the goal of completely banning commercial trade of those species whose survival is threatened by extinction in the absence of strict regulations.[92]

The convention banned international trading of Brazilian rosewood timber, while the export of Afrormosia, an African timber, needs permits. It put regulations on the trade of tigers and other big cats, Asian rhinos, monkeys, orchids, and parrots. The rapid decline in the number of elephants, blue whales, and other large animals represents the overexploitation of

Figure 8.1   Elephants were among those animals that the Convention on International Trade in Endangered Species of Wild Fauna and Flora were most intended to protect. The convention came into force in 1973 with the goal of completely banning the commercial trade of those species whose survival is completely threatened by extinction.

nature (Figure 8.1). African elephants were killed for the ivory in their tusks. More than 80 percent of ivory products were imported by Japan. Measures to ban trade in ivory were enacted under heavy pressure from NGOs, the United States, and the European Community at the 1989 CITES conference. The ban reduced incentives for poaching African elephants, with a resultant plunge in world raw ivory prices.

While CITES focuses on preventing the extinction of territorial wildlife, concerns with birds and other migratory species resulted in such international treaties as the 1979 Convention on the Conservation of Migratory Species of Wild Animals. The treaty recognizes wild animals as an irreplaceable part of the earth's natural system. It was designed to prevent the killing of migratory species, and to remove obstacles to their migration, and to control other factors that might endanger them. States are obliged to maintain wetlands and other habitats for those migratory species.[93]

The International Convention for the Regulation of Whaling followed publicity on the plight of whales, which suffered from a long history of overhunting that threatened their extinction. The International Whaling Commission created by the 1946 Convention helped establish strict quotas on the number of whales to be caught annually and their minimum sizes along with the prohibition of hunting certain species near extinction. These regulations, however, were not effective until a moratorium on banning all commercial whaling began to be implemented in 1986.

In 1994, the pressure from anti-whaling groups led to the creation of a whale sanctuary in the Southern Ocean and Antarctica. These measures were resisted mostly by Norway, Japan, and Iceland, who wanted to protect their minor economic interests. These countries began so-called scientific whaling after the international convention stopped commercial whaling activities. In particular, Norway openly defied the ban by killing 226 mink whales in 1993 to satisfy domestic whaling interest groups (Figure 8.2).

ENFORCEMENT OF RULES

Given the interconnectedness of environmental issues across borders, national governments need to agree on international treaties and arrangements that facilitate policy coordination. Because the treaties are binding only on those who agree to them,

Figure 8.2   The international convention stopped commercial whaling in 1986. These efforts were resisted by Norway, Japan, and Iceland who wanted to protect their minor economic interests. In 1993, Norway openly defied the ban by killing 226 minke whales (Antarctic, or Southern Minke Whale, shown above) to satisfy domestic whaling interest groups in that country.

their effectiveness depends on the involvement of as many countries as possible. Since abiding by international treaties may not be a government's main priority, monitoring activities become very important.

It is one thing to produce, through active negotiations, regulations for the protection of the atmosphere, preservation of biological diversity and the natural habitat, and the control of air pollution. It is another to develop an enforcement mechanism to change the behavior of polluters. Since the national governments of polluters are not easily forced to adopt required environmental standards, pubic pressure and support are necessary in order for countries to fulfil their international obligations.

9

Global Institutions and Civil Society

Environmental deterioration can be tackled at various levels. The
implementation of environmental policies requires the participation
of diverse actors, ranging from non-governmental organizations
(NGOs) and national governments to international organizations.
While local communities must be involved in preserving the wealth
of their natural environment, global coordination is essential to
protect biodiversity and wildlife habitat, reduce global warming,
and stop the depletion of the ozone layer, all of which have an
impact on everyone on the planet.

INTERNATIONAL ORGANIZATIONS AND COORDINATION
International organizations are engaged in coordinating efforts to
harmonize different national standards and regulations. They also

provide independent sources of information and analysis of the growing environmental abuse. International organizations facilitate environmental agreement by serving as a forum for negotiation and by offering technical assistance.

The **United Nations Environmental Programme** (UNEP), headquartered in Kenya, was created explicitly to survey and monitor the global environmental situations and management.[94] One of the UNEP's primary tasks has been the development of a body of knowledge about the global environment by conducting scientific assessments on rates of desertification, deforestation, air pollution, ozone depletion, and the loss of biological diversity. These data are used in harmonizing different environmental standards and setting guidelines for the management of environmental resources.

Beyond providing information about environmental quality, the UNEP finances the protection of tropical forests, wildlife preservation, and other projects. In collaboration with the World Wildlife Fund (WWF) and the International Union for the Conservation of Nature and Natural Resources (IUCN), the UNEP launched the World Conservation Strategy in 1980. The strategy is aimed at preserving genetic diversity and ensuring the sustainable utilization of species and ecosystems.

Other organizations focus on single or few specific issues such as global warming and the protection of endangered species. The World Meteorological Organization conducts scientific research and is engaged in monitoring global climate changes. The International Maritime Organization is concerned with reduction in pollution through overseeing shipping activities. The International Tropical Timber Organization has been involved in facilitating an agreement to ensure that all the tropical timber is produced by well-managed forests. The United Nations Educational, Scientific, and Cultural Organization (UNESCO) has been facilitating scientific research and environmental education since its founding in 1945. In 1968, it organized the first international Conference on the

Biosphere and in 1971 launched the Man and Biosphere (MAB) Programme, which is designed to provide information on wildlife conservation.

The UN agencies can perform a central function in coordinating activities in specific areas. The International Tropical Timber Organization was formed to protect the future of timber trade and conserve the forest ecosystem. The UN Food and Agricultural Organization (FAO) plays a monitoring and advisory role on forest management. In collaboration with the UNEP and UNESCO, the FAO promotes the Tropical Forest Action Plan, which was designed to slow down deforestation. The FAO also coordinates, through its regional fisheries commissions, programs to increase fisheries management capacity in developing countries.

The World Meteorological Organization (WMO), concerned with long-term climate changes, sponsored the First World Climate Conference in 1979 and the Second World Climate Conference in 1990.[95] These meetings contributed to the consolidation of scientific consensus on global warming and drew the attention of policy makers to the issue. The Intergovernmental Panel on Climate Change, created under the co-sponsorship of the WMO and UNEP, produced a critical assessment report in 1995 that noted a discernable human influence on the climate. In the atmospheric policy area, the WMO marshals monitoring systems and scientific expertise.[96]

International organizations provide technical support for reduction in emissions of greenhouse gases and preservation of resources.[97] Technical and scientific advice is available to countries combating transboundary environmental threats to the atmosphere, biodiversity, and water resources.

INTERNATIONAL FUNDING

Along with technical support, external funding has been earmarked for environmental projects that benefit the global environment. International funding has supported the transfer of environmentally sound technologies for climate control and biodiversity. The Global Environmental Facility (GEF) was institutionalized at the 1992 summit in Rio de Janeiro in order to funnel loans to low-income countries. While the World Bank is in control over financial assistance programs, the GEF has also been sponsored by the UN Environmental Programme (UNEP).

The GEF and other financial mechanisms are dedicated to support measures that involve providing funding for developing countries to implement environmental agreements.[98] In the case of the Montreal Protocol on Substances that Deplete the Ozone Layer, its Multilateral Fund has supported reductions in the consumption of ozone-depleting substances in Eastern Europe, Central Asia, and other countries that are poor or in economically difficult situations.

The implementation of global and regional agreements on the protection and restoration of freshwater and marine ecosystems has benefited from GEF-supported activities. In collaboration with the UNDP, the GEF supported the Black Sea Convention and the Danube River Protection Convention, which are agreements designed to reduce pollution and improve resource management. The funding helped the governments of Turkey, Bulgaria, Romania, Georgia, Russia, Ukraine, and their ten upstream neighbors restore the Danube River/Black Sea basin plagued by excessive levels of municipal and industrial wastewater release as well as agricultural pesticides and other wastes.

The GEF also approved over $1.2 billion in grants and leveraged $6 billion in co-financing of more than 100 clean energy projects in 60 countries that are interested in the use of renewable energy technologies. Fuel-cell buses that run on hydrogen and emit only distilled water have been introduced to replace diesel buses in several large cities in developing countries. This project aims at reducing local air pollution and the accumulation of carbon dioxide in the atmosphere.

Another area, supported by international funding, focused on community-based conservation within protected areas. As part of efforts to reverse the degradation of high-altitude pastures and forest stands, the GEF extended its support to ecological landscape management. Biodiversity projects were approved to improve the management of four conservancies with a representative sample of biomes in the highest mountain ranges of the Western Himalayas and Hindu Kush.

The GEF Small Grants Programme offers up to $50,000 directly to more than 700 non-governmental and community-based organizations. The program has funded over 3,400 projects in more than 60 countries in support of conserving and restoring the natural world. In particular, these funding programs have been geared toward empowering local people who are engaged in rehabilitating land that has been degraded by cyclical droughts, arid cultivation, and the depletion of forest cover for fuel wood.

NON-GOVERNMENTAL ORGANIZATIONS

Since the emergence of ecological concerns in the late 1960s, the role of non-governmental organizations (NGOs) has become increasingly visible.[99] **Environmental movements**, both local and global, have been pressing policy makers to recognize their concerns as well as appealing to the public. Numerous groups exist, ranging from Himalayan village associations protesting deforestation to a worldwide network of groups campaigning against global warming, destruction of wetland and other habitats, killings of whales, and loss of wildlife.

Large national and international NGOs suggest new policy initiatives, gather information, offer scientific advice, and lobby to promote strict standards on control of climate change and protection of endangered species. In addition, the NGOs can organize protests and boycotts, produce educational merchandise, and carry out scientific research.

In order to appeal to the public conscience and engender moral sensitivities, NGOs such as Greenpeace, Friends of the Earth, and Earth First sometimes take direct action. By documenting the

Figure 9.1   Dozens of Greenpeace activists lie in protest demonstrating outside Mexico's foreign ministry on June 7, 2001. They were protesting Mexico's support for a proposal to resume commercial whaling by laying in a line to represent a giant whale's tail.

scenes of killing whales, Greenpeace drew media attention and generated a worldwide sensation (Figure 9.1). On the other hand, NGOs such as the Sierra Club, National Wildlife Federation, Nature Conservancy, Audubon Society, Environmental Defense Fund, and the Wilderness Society are more interested in lobbying governments directly than in organizing protests. Some of them have been involved in helping indebted countries such as Bolivia, Ecuador, Zambia, and Madagascar reduce their international loans in return for preserving a large proportion of their forests and land for wildlife conservation.[100]

Whatever the philosophies and methods, the ultimate aim of the environmental movement is to maintain the quality of the ecological system. NGOs hold governments and businesses accountable through their information gathering and other monitoring activities.

The role of NGOs is significant especially since there is no central enforcement authority in an international system. Through their watchdog role, NGOs press countries to enforce international agreements. NGO monitoring reports can reveal environmentally harmful activities that the government may have not been aware of. By forming a coalition in specific issue areas such as the protection of rain forests, NGOs can win broad social approval for their agendas.

NGOs are in a unique position to link public interest to global and national environmental policymaking and implementation. Professional organizations such as the International Union for the Conservation of Nature and Natural Resources (IUCN) utilize a scientific knowledge base for mobilizing political support. IUCN was founded in 1948 to monitor the state of living resources for conservation purposes. In coordination with the International Council for Bird Preservation, the IUCN publishes a set of books containing all the available information of the endangered plant and animal species. These "Red Lists" identify threatened animal and plant species.

The IUCN Wildlife Trade Monitoring Unit is supported by voluntary offices around the world in studying and, if possible, halting the commercial sale of wild animal species. Along with the World Wildlife Fund (WWF), created in 1961, the IUCN has also accepted administrative responsibilities for the Convention on International Trade in Endangered Species of Fauna and Flora. The World Wildlife Funds supported tiger conservation projects in India by helping the government set aside a series of wildlife preserves.

Many NGOs are working on conservation issues: rain forest conservation is supported by Rainforest Alliance (based in New York) and Rainforest Concern (located in London), both of which identify and organize activities to protect threatened tropical rain forest. Save the Redwoods League (based in San Francisco) has been engaged in protecting the remaining giant redwood trees growing in California forests. Very few wilderness areas are left that do not allow the use of cars, motorboats, snowmobiles, motorcycles, and planes. The Wilderness Society attempts to protect these areas from logging, mining and oil drilling companies as well as those who use motors for convenience or sports.

The Fauna and Flora Preservation Society was involved in saving the white oryx of the Arabian Desert from the brink of extinction. The group was also organizing educational programs on the value of the mountain gorillas of the Virunga volcanoes that straddle the borders of Rwanda, Zaire, and Uganda in Central Africa; the number of the gorillas declined to less than 350, and they need to be protected from poaching (Figure 9.2). The British-based Whale and Dolphin Conservation Society campaigns for the protection of whales, dolphins, and porpoises around the globe.

NGOs complement international organizations in scientific research and policy formulation. With the support of UNEP and UNESCO, the International Council of Scientific Unions (ICSU), a federation of organizations of natural sciences, formed the Scientific Committee on Problems of the Environment to study the impact of human activities on biochemical changes on the planet. NGOs have been involved in setting up air pollution standards in Europe, in support of the European Union's efforts to reduce greenhouse gas emissions.

A coalition made up of NGOs played a particularly important role in preventing large-scale exploitation of marine resources and internal development in the Antarctic by urging states to respect the Antarctic Treaty signed in 1959. The Antarctic and Southern Ocean Coalition (ASOC), established in 1978, represents a worldwide association of over 200 non-governmental organizations, including Friends of the Earth, Greenpeace, and the International Union for the Conservation of Nature. In the early 1980s, Greenpeace and other environmental groups began to lobby to protect the wilderness from mining and other resource-extracting activities that endanger the fragile ecosystem in Antarctica. Their efforts were supported by the 1991 Environmental Protocol that prohibits mineral exploration for at least 50 years and

Figure 9.2   The number of mountain gorillas living in the
four national parks that straddle Uganda, Zaire, and Rwanda
in Central Africa had declined to less that 350, but after the
International Gorilla Conservation Programme was established,
their numbers are slowly increasing. Still, only about 700 of them
remain. The primary threat to their survival is forest clearance
and degradation, but many are killed by poachers.

establishes a framework for preserving the continent as a world park.

LOCAL COMMUNITIES

In tropical forests, millions of indigenous populations have lived for thousands of years, obtaining their food by hunting and gathering and growing crops. In some tropical rain forests, the original indigenous inhabitants have lived in the same place for generations. The Yanomami Indians of Orinoco River Basin in Venezuela remain the largest group of rainforest inhabitants in South America. Some of them were not known to the outside world until the 1950s. In the rain forests of Sarawak, Malaysia, located on the island of Borneo, most dwellers are nomadic, hunting wild pigs using blowpipes made out of palm stems as well as collecting precious woods, nuts, and resins.

These rainforest communities are vulnerable to those who seek to exploit their resources. Tribal communities lack the political and economic influence necessary to fight the system imposed on them. However, struggles against building big dams and logging of primary forests are visible in many parts of the world.

Many settlers have been encouraged to move into the rain forests by the governments of Brazil and Indonesia. In Indonesia, over one million people moved from the island of Java to less inhabited islands. The Polonoroeste project in Brazil allowed a huge influx of people to settle in the rain forest as part of the government population program. This led to the rapid deforestation of parts of the rain forest and created severe social conflicts.

Indigenous people's way of life will disappear along with the destruction of their rain forests. Local struggles to save rain forests often takes place between loggers, ranchers, and farmers on one side and indigenous people on the other. The Awa people in the rain forests of Ecuador and Columbia cut down a strip of the rain forest around their area to curb the penetration of invaders who want to spoil their land.

Environmental and human rights groups have recognized the marginalized situations of indigenous tribal groups who live in forests and have helped to mobilize public support. Local coalition groups have been formed in support of indigenous struggles against the destruction of rain forests in Indonesia and Malaysia. As part of an international campaign, the Japan Tropical Forest Action Network supported children and women of communities affected by logging and commercial agricultural schemes in Sarawak. They also called for preventing the importation of tropical timber.

In order to protect the rain forests, rubber tappers of the western Amazon have opposed the cutting and burning of forests for roads and ranches. The tappers rely on the forest for their livelihood, collecting sap from rubber trees without harming the trees and gathering nuts in seasons when the rubber is not flowing. They have struggled with wealthy ranchers by using such tactics as thwarting the ranchers' chain-saw crews. While their struggle drew international support, Chico Mendes, a leader of the rubber tappers was shot and killed by ranchers in December 1988.

In Costa Rica, the timber industry is responsible for 90 percent of forest destruction. Environmental groups have encouraged local communities to keep forests under their control by holding on to their land. They have taught local people sustainable ways of harvesting wood without destroying the forest as well as developing regional markets for their products.

Tree-growing activities have been popular with rural women who live in impoverished communities. Women's organizations in Zimbabwe, Namibia, and Kenya have been involved in reintroducing traditional seeds and indigenous tree species to reverse soil erosion (Figure 9.3). The movements promote traditional agricultural techniques that were previously abandoned in favor of modern farming methods that rely on fertilizers, pesticides, new seed varieties, and irrigation systems.

Figure 9.3 Nobel Peace Prize winner Wangari Maathai, a Kenyan environmentalist, is the first African woman to win this award for aiding the continent's poor with a campaign to plant millions of trees to slow down deforestation.

Indigenous fishing communities suffer from the depletion of fisheries in their waters mainly due to the activities of foreign fleets. Driftnet fishing and other modern forms of destructive fishing by other countries have an impact on daily survival in the South Pacific Islands. Communities of the Pacific have been waging international campaigns to persuade China and Japan to withdraw their fleets. Their campaigns have not been very successful due to the high profitability of irresponsible fishing activities and the disregard of the two countries for international laws.

⑩

The Choices for
Future Generations

*In our way of life . . . with every decision we make, we always
keep in mind the Seventh Generation of children to come. . . .
When we walk upon Mother Earth, we always plant our feet
carefully, because we know that the faces of future generations are looking up at us from beneath the ground. We never
forget them.*

—Oren Lyons, Faithkeeper,
Onondaga Nation, Earth Day 1993 pledge

The sustainable use of natural resources flows from understanding the richness
of complex ecosystems and how people can live in harmony with them.
The native people regard the land, water, plants, and animals as part
of one unified and interdependent whole. In making any change in
nature, they carefully consider its likely impact not only in the imme-
diate future but also upon their children and children's children.

People's perceptions of the environment are essential elements of
cultural identity. Fifty million indigenous people, living in tropical rain
forests, know how to identify and use plants for food and medicine.
Since they know how to use the forest without destroying it, the
survival of indigenous peoples is the key to the future preservation
of natural forests. Their right to live in the rain forests ought to be
respected and supported.

In mainstream culture, humans are separated from their environment, since nature is viewed as a resource to exploit for profit. However, a high quality of life would not be possible without the existence of a healthy and productive environment.

The human dimensions of globalization have been influenced by powerful images of automobiles, television, clothing, and other consumer goods shown on the global media. The dream of the good life, as characterized by material possessions, is increasingly shared by people worldwide. This version of human life based on endless material expansion cannot be sustained forever on a limited planet.

The transition to a globalized world has become a reality, yet transition to a sustainable one is far from certain. Cars, airplanes, and other conveniences are part of modern life, but the pollution created by them causes harm to our health (Figure 10.1). The atmosphere is filled with harmful gases. The rivers and oceans are polluted. Natural forests are vanishing quickly. The health of the planet and of human welfare are threatened by growing pollution, continuing deforestation, water scarcity, and increasing toxic waste and rubbish, along with a rapidly expanding population.

Our immense responsibility stems from an awareness of the ecological damage caused by humans. Unfortunately, many decisions made today by our governments and corporations take very short-term perspectives. The long-term effects of global environmental changes are very difficult to reverse over the period of one generation. By not taking effective global action, we are now plundering our children's future in an unprecedented way.

Natural capital assets are running down rapidly with the decline of nearly two-thirds of ecological services. According to a report of the Millennium Ecosystem Assessment, a UN organization that focuses on the benefits people obtain from ecosystems, "In many cases, it is literally a matter of living on borrowed time." [101] More land has been changed for crop

Figure 10.1 Traffic drives toward downtown Los Angeles on the 110 Freeway as a curtain of smog shrouds the skyline on July 21, 1998. After 6 years of decreasing smog levels, smog was making a comeback.

production since 1945 than in the previous two centuries combined. Since the 1980s, the quantity of fish caught by humans has been declining because of a shortage of stock resulting from overfishing. Fresh water supplies are being withdrawn far faster than being recharged. While natural resources are being used up quicker than they can be replenished, greenhouse gas emissions will continue to grow with the increasing use of fossil fuel.

There is a "window of opportunity" to preserve the world's high-biodiversity wilderness areas, important marine regions, and coral reef hotspots before they disappear forever. UN research warns of threats to the delicate ecological balance on three-quarters of the earth's total land surface within the next 30 years.[102]

Unless there is a drastic change, time is limited. Pollution and ecological destruction increase in tandem with the expansion of the world economy. Responding to environmental degradation is slower than economic growth.

Effective approaches must encompass measures based not only on science but also on an ethical basis. How we act today will have an enormous impact on tomorrow's environment.[103] Our knowledge, emotional energy, motivation, time, and monetary resources should be channeled toward conservation. Since global environmental challenges cut across economic sectors beyond one geographical region, they cannot be effectively handled issue by issue or by a small number of countries.

As individuals, we can each make changes to our lifestyles, acting with real motivation and determination to preserve our environment. Many decisions made by ordinary people regarding the conduct of their daily life put an undue pressure on the ecological system to be shared with other species and the amount and type of waste produced. **Earth Day** has been held annually on April 22 to enhance awareness of the key environmental issues of water, sustainable consumption and production, and renewable energy and climate change (Figure 10.2). Fairs, rallies, and conferences are organized across the world to

Figure 10.2 Earth Day is held annually on April 22. Venezuelan street performers, representing the Earth, at left, and Industrialization, at right, demonstrate in downtown Caracas. Local environmental groups marched during the celebration of Earth Day in 1999.

mobilize local action. One campaign asks the public to make "one small change" in their daily lives such as a pledge to reuse plastic bags and turn off the tap during tooth brushing.

ECOLOGICAL LIVING

We need to do more to integrate sustainable living into our daily routines. This means more recycling, increased use of solar energy, increased consumption of more natural food products, and preservation of rain forests. Recycling, recovering, and using glass, paper, plastics, and metals again are essential to conserving precious natural resources and managing waste. The 2000 Olympic Games in Sydney, Australia, dramatically represented environmental thinking in that the site of the Olympic Park stadium itself was converted from a contaminated industrial wasteland (Figure 10.3).

Figure 10.3 Fireworks explode during the opening ceremony of the Rugby World Cup in 2003. The ethos of environmental thinking was dramatically represented by the site for this stadium, which was converted from a contaminated industrial wasteland.

Recycling and reuse of many products help preserve critical ecosystems. Plastic is made from oil or coal; car bodies are made of steel, produced from iron ore. The rain forests have been disturbed by mining companies. The roads built by them allow more people through to ravage the wild habitat for cattle farming and other purposes.

Overconsumption, along with the unnecessary production of goods and services, can be reduced with the prevention of subsidies that encourage individuals and companies to be wasteful. In Denmark, imposing a tax on waste resulted in increased recycling.

Public transit can be made more viable by reducing reliance on single-passenger vehicles. Since approximately 60 percent of oil consumption is devoted to transportation, walking, bike riding, or carpooling reduce carbon dioxide (CO_2) emissions. Driving 15 miles less a week decreases approximately 780 pounds of CO_2 a year. Higher vehicle and fuel taxes can be imposed to encourage the use of public transportation. For example, Norway has a toll ring system in three cities that charges a fee for motorized entry to cities.

Undertaking climate change involves more gain than pain, since cleaner air and less traffic congestion are beneficial to us. Pollution can be reduced by the use of better technology in our cars, trucks, and SUVs. In the wake of rising fuel prices and increased concerns over global warming, consumers are increasingly turning to hybrid cars. The unexpected popularity of such energy-efficient cars has helped influence public policy through tax breaks and access to express lanes for hybrid owners.

Energy use can be reduced through taxes on the industrial and commercial use of energy. Such a "climate change levy" is necessary to support a switch to pollution-free technology. Many of the 2 billion people living in rural Third World communities will be able to take advantage of solar energy with the help of industries involved in solar cell manufacturing. Loans and other incentives can be provided to assist farmers in repairing leaks and switching to more efficient irrigation systems.

WHAT WE CAN DO

We can cut down waste by reusing and recycling paper, glass, bottle, jars, plastics, cans, textiles, and wood. We can save unwanted clothes, books and other goods for thrift stores and purchase from them as well. We can avoid disposable cameras, paper plates, and other goods that are thrown away immediately after use. We can buy high-quality recycled products that can last for a lifetime.

Consumer products, such as televisions, fridges, ranges, and computers can be repaired and reused instead of thrown away. Fruit, vegetable peelings, and other organic waste can be composted instead of dumped in landfills. We have to be vigilant in responsibly discarding paints, batteries, medicines, garden chemicals, and other dangerous toxic materials often included in household chemicals.

Since nearly one-third of the trash in landfills in the United States and other industrialized countries comes from over-packaging, avoiding the purchase of over-packaged goods and the excessive use of paper will lead to a reduction in our waste. Buy food and drinks in returnable containers.

Instead of plastic shopping bags, we should take our own backpack or canvas bag. Plastic bags can be used again. Plastic bags floating in rivers and oceans unnecessarily kill wildlife. A whale that died off the coast of France in 2002 had 364 pounds of plastic bags in his stomach. Such bags can be mistaken for jellyfish and other animals that other sea life feed on.

Saving electricity helps reduce greenhouse gases, because most electricity is produced by burning fossil fuels that release carbon dioxide. Turning off lights, televisions, and computers when not in use saves a significant amount of electricity. We can save electricity by avoiding excessive dependence on air conditioners and turning heat down. Standard lightbulbs can be replaced by compact fluorescent lights.

Water-saving measures include turning off the faucet during tooth brushing and avoiding leaving the water running during dish washing. Other slight changes in daily habits such as shutting all the faucets tightly may look insignificant, but can make a huge difference if everyone acted accordingly.

People can lobby their political representatives, write to media, and talk to the industries and shops about measures to reduce waste and greenhouse gas emissions, and protect rain forests. Such campaigns can include boycotting furniture or other goods made from rainforest timber, such as mahogany or teak, in support of plantation-grown timber or second-hand timber. Boycotts can also be organized against companies that produce poisonous waste that pollutes the world's oceans, lakes, and rivers.

LOCAL ACTION

Below are examples of actions taken by youth. Children across North America wrote letters to fishing companies to catch tuna in such a way as not to harm dolphins, which are often killed by their nets. This action resulted in the introduction of the dolphin-safe tuna label by companies who adopt fishing methods that do not endanger dolphins.

Students in a Massachusetts middle school collected 4,000 signatures to lobby for a state law that mandates packaging juice and other beverages in glass bottles with a return deposit. In addition to the deposit project, the students also started to work on a law to reduce extra packaging.

A group of children in Helsinki, Finland, have introduced solar cookers to schools in Namibia so that they do not need to collect firewood. Every year, they take cookers designed by the best Finnish solar engineers to Namibia and show Namibian young people how to use the cookers themselves.

OUR RESPONSIBILITIES

By understanding that humanity is an integral part of a much larger whole, we can define our role neither separate from nor in opposition to nature. By recognizing that all parts of nature have an inherent right to exist, we will be able to find more "comfort and delight from the diversity of nature and the miracles of life."[104] Nature's beauty has been expressed in art, literature, poetry, music, songs, and dance for millennia. The privilege of admiring the wonders of nature should be a perpetual right for every generation to come. In the words of Queen Noor of Jordan, "It is our solemn duty to ensure that they, like us, can benefit from its bounty and enjoy its richness." [105]

Biological diversity (biodiversity)—The rich variety of life forms in nature and their interdependence, which is essential to maintaining a fragile ecological system.

Deforestation—The destruction of forests by large-scale logging. Tropical rain forests, which are home to over half the plant and animal species on earth, vanish too quickly.

Earth Day—Yearly fairs, rallies, and conferences organized across the world on April 22 to enhance the awareness of such environmental issues as sustainable consumption and production, renewable energy, climate change, and biological diversity.

Ecological footprint—An ecological footprint is a measure of how much land and water is needed to produce the resources we consume and to dispose of the waste we produce. Footprint analysis helps us measure the biologically productive area required for maintaining our life.

Environmental conflict—Conflict arises from competition for limited or inequitably distributed land, fresh water, and other natural resources needed for survival of a given population. In particular, soil erosion and shortage of water, along with overpopulation, aggravate the conditions for conflict.

Environmental movements—Organizations such as Greenpeace, Friends of the Earth, Defenders of Wildlife, and the World Wildlife Fund, that have been protesting deforestation, destruction of habitats, killings of endangered species, and loss of wildlife as well as campaigning against global warming.

Global warming—The increased level of carbon dioxide, methane, and other gases in the atmosphere that results in heating up the earth's atmosphere through the greenhouse effect. Heat is trapped in the atmosphere by the build-up of the above gases released from car exhausts and the burning of fossil fuels in factories and power stations.

Globalization—The trend towards a single, integrated, and interdependent world. In an environmental context, globalization reflects both the prehistoric and historic tendency of the human species to expand their activities.

Overfishing—The harvesting of a fish species to the point where it can no longer reproduce itself in large numbers in a given area. In the world oceans, increasingly not enough fish are left to breed. Many fish species, such as cod, have been over-caught by the modern fishing industry, which uses sonar devices to locate shoals of fish as well as a variety of lines, traps, and nets.

Sustainable development—Development that meets the needs of the present generation without sacrificing the ability to meet the needs of future generations.

United Nations Environmental Programme—A UN agency that is engaged in monitoring the rates of desertification, deforestation, air pollution, ozone depletion, loss of species, and other environmentally critical areas. Its data are used to set international guidelines for a sustainable management of ecological systems.

1. James Gustave Speth, *Red Sky at Morning: America and the Crisis of the Global Environment*. New Haven: Yale University Press, 2004, p. 11.

2. Ibid., p. 21.

3. Preston Gralla, *How the Environment Works*. Emeryville, CA: Ziff-David Press, 1994, p. x.

4. Speth, *Red Sky at Morning*, p. 21.

5. Elizabeth Dowswell, "Production and Consumption." *Our Planet*, 2003. Available online at http://www.ourplanet.com.

6. Gary Gardner, et al., "The State of Consumption Today," *State of the World*, Worldwatch Institute. New York: W. W. Norton & Company, 2004, p. 4.

7. Ibid.

8. Ibid.

9. Speth, *Red Sky at Morning*, p. 21.

10. Ibid.

11. Jean-Francois Rischard, *High Noon: 20 Global Problems, 20 Years to Solve Them*. New York: Basic Books, 2002, pp. 74-75.

12. Janet L. Sawin, "Making Better Energy Choices," *State of the World*, Worldwatch Institute. New York: W. W. Norton & Company, 2004, pp. 24–43.

13. S. Spray and K.L. McGlothin, *Global Climate Change*. New York: Rowman and Littlefield Publishing Inc., 2002.

14. Michael Collier and Robert Webb, *Floods, Droughts, and Climate Change*. Tucson, AZ: University of Arizona Press, 2002.

15. J. Griffin, *Global Climate Change*. UK: Edward Elgar Publishing, 2003.

16. BBC, "In Depth: Global Warming?" Available online at http://news.bbc.co.uk.

17. David Burnie, *Earth Watch*. New York: Dorling Kindersley, 2001.

18. Brian Groombridge and Martin D Jenkins, *World Atlas of Biodiversity*. Berkeley, CA: University of California Press, 2002.

19. Jagdish Koonjul, "Small Is Vulnerable." In "Special Theme Issue: Seas, Oceans and Small Islands," *Our Planet*, 2004.

20. Lian Pin Koh et al., "Species Coextinctions and the Biodiversity Crisis." *Science* (September 2004).

21. J. A. Thomas, et al., "Comparative Losses of British Butterflies, Birds, and Plants and the Global Extinction Crisis." *Science* (March 2004).

22. Norman Myers, "What's This Biodiversity and What's It Done for Us Today?" *The Biodiversity Crisis*, ed. Michael J. Novacek. New York: The New Press, 2000.

23. Burnie, *Earth Watch*.

24. RainforestWeb.Org. Available online at http://www.rainforestweb.org/Rainforest_Information/Biodiversity.

25. Rainforest Action Network, 2005. Available online at http://www.ran.org.

26. Spencer R. Weart, *The Discovery of Global Warming*. Cambridge, MA: Harvard University Press, 2003.

27. R. Lester Brown, *Eco-Economy: Building an Economy for the Earth*. New York: W. W. Norton & Company, 2001.

28. World fisheries capture from the wild amounted to 93.2 million tons in 2002; China's catches amounted to 20 percent of total world capture.

29. United Nations Environmental Programme, *Tunza: Acting for a Better World*, 2003. Available online at http://www.ourplanet.com/tunza.

30. Brian Groombridge and Martin D. Jenkins, *The World Atlas of Biodiversity: Earth's Living Resources in the 21st Century*. Los Angeles: University of California Press, 2002.

31. Melanie L. Stiassny, "Case Study: Lake Victoria," *The Biodiversity Crisis*, ed. Michael J. Novacek. New York: The New Press, 2000.

32. Hama Arba Diallo, "Regaining Ground," Special Theme Issue: Global Environmental Facility, *Our Planet*, 2003. Available online at http://www.ourplanet.com.

33. United Nations Environmental Programme, United Nations Development Programme, The World Bank, and World Resources Institute, *2002–2004 World Resources: Decisions for the Earth: Balance, Voice, and Power.* Washington D.C.: World Resource Institute, 2003.

34. Peter Swanson, *Water, the Drop of Life.* Minnetonka, MN: NorthWord Press, 2001.

35. Burnie, *Earth Watch.*

36. United Nations Educational, Scientific, and Cultural Organization, *International Year of Fresh Water: Facts and Figures: Desertification and Drought*, 2003. http://www.wateryear2003.org.

37. Kenneth M. Vigil, *Clean Water: An Introduction to Water Quality and Water Pollution Control*, 2nd ed. Corvallis, OR: Oregon State University Press, 2003.

38. Swanson, *Water, the Drop of Life*, p. 125.

39. Ibid., p. 12.

40. World Bank, *World Development Report 2004.* Washington D.C.: World Bank and Oxford University Press, 2003.

41. Burnie, *Earth Watch.*

42. U.S. Census Bureau. *Global Population Profile 2002.* Available online at www.census.gov/ipc/www/wp02.html.

43. United Nations Environmental Programme, *Global Environmental Outlook-3 (GEO-3)*, 2002. http://www.unep.org/geo/geo3/

44. Nicky Chambers, Craig Simmons, and Mathis Wackernagel, *Sharing Nature's Interest: Ecological Footprints as an Indicator of Sustainability.* Sterling, VA: Earthscan Publishing, 2000.

45. WWF International, *The Living Planet Report 2004*, 5th ed. Gland, Switzerland, WWF: 2004

46. United Nations Environmental Programme, *Tunza: Acting for a Better World.*

47. Maarten Messiaen, "Environment: Global North's 'Ecological Footprint' Dwarfs South's." *Global Information Network* (October 22, 2004).

48. Paul Harrison, *American Association for the Advancement of Science Atlas of Population and Environment.* Los Angeles: University of California Press, 2001.

49. Global Footprint Network 2005. Available online at http://www.footprintnetwork.org.

50. WWF International, *The Living Planet Report.*

51. WWF, *Living Planet Report* 2002.

52. Ibid.

53. *Ode*, vol. 3, no. 4, May 2005, p. 11.

54. Samuel Stucki and Christian Ludwig, "Introduction," *Municipal Solid Waste Management*, ed. Christian Ludwig et al. Berlin: Springer, 2003, p. 10.

55. Government of Japan, Fundamental Plan for Establishing a Sound Material-Cycle Society, March 2003. Available online at http://www.env. go.jp/en/pol/wemj/basicplan.pdf.

56. Stucki and Ludwig, "Introduction."

57. Richard Anthony, "Reduce, Reuse, Recycle: The Zero Waste Approach," *Municipal Solid Waste Management*, ed. Christian Ludwig et al. Berlin: Springer, 2003, pp. 46–65.

58. Ibid., p. 46.

59. Stucki and Ludwig, "Introduction," p. 11.

60. Anthony, "Reduce, Reuse, Recycle," p. 47.

61. Ibid., p. 61.

62. James A. Listorti and Fadi M. Doumani, "Environmental Health: Bridging the Gaps." World Bank Discussion Paper, No. 422, 2001.

63. The Basel Convention remains the broadest and most serious international treaty on the transboundary movement. After being adopted in the early 1990s, 117 countries, plus the European Community, have been committed to supporting environmentally sound disposal of hazardous wastes.

64. Swanson, *Water, the Drop of Life.*

65. United Nations Environmental Programme, *Global Environmental Outlook-3 (GEO-3)*, 2002.

66. Kefyn M. Catley, "Global Warming, Loss of Habitat, and Pollution: Introduction to 'Thompson's Ice Corps,' 'Nest Gains, Nest Losses', and 'Hormonal Sabotage'," *The Biodiversity Crisis: Losing What Counts*, ed. Michael Novacek. New York: New Press, 2001, pp. 100–106.

67. *Environment*, September 2003, vol. 45, no. 10, p. 24.

68. Thilo Bode, "Sea Changes", *Our Planet*, 2003. Available online at http://www.ourplanet.com.

69. United Nations Environmental Programme, *Global Environmental Outlook-3.*

70. Ibid.

71. Ibid.

72. Ibid.

73. Ian Johnson and Kseniya Lvovsky, "World Bank Special: Double Burden", *Our Planet*, 2003. Available online at http://www.ourplanet.com

74. Mark Malloch Brown, "Empowering the Poor," *Our Planet*, 2003. Available online at http://www.ourplanet.com.

75. Ibid.

76. United Nations Environmental Programme, United Nations Development Programme, The World Bank, and World Resources Institute, *2002–2004 World Resources: Decisions for the Earth*. Washington, D.C.: World Resource Institute, 2003.

77. P. O'Keefe, "Biomass Burning in Rural Homes in Tropical Areas," *Encyclopedia of Global Environmental Change*, vol. 3. New York: John Wiley and Sons Publishing, 2002.

78. Partha Dasgupta, "Taking the Measure of Unsustainability," *Our Planet*, 2003. Available online at http://www.ourplanet.com.

79. Antony Burgmans, "Cooperation is Catching," *Our Planet*, 2003. Available online at http://www.ourplanet.com/

80. O'Keefe, "Biomass Burning in Rural Homes in Tropical Areas."

81. Concerns have been raised with wind energy, since wind propellers often kill many birds, including endangered species.

82. Jose Goldenberg, "Critical Energy," *Our Planet*, 2003. Available online at http://www.ourplanet.com.

83. Leonard Good, "Brightening the Future," Our Planet, 2003. Available online at http://www.ourplanet.com.

84. Paula Berinstein, *Alternative Energy: Facts, Statistics, and Issues*. Westport, CT: Oryx Press, 2001.

85. Pew Center, *Global Climate Change*, 2004. Arlington, VA. Available online at www.pewclimate.org.

86. Swanson, *Water, the Drop of Life.*

87. Polly Ghazi, "Waste Not," *Our Planet*, 2003. Available online at http://www.ourplanet.com

88. Diane Raines Ward, *Water Wars*, New York: Riverhead Books, 2002.

89. The World Summit on Sustainable Development (WSSD) was held in Johannesburg, South Africa, from 26 August to 4 September 2002 to reaffirm the declarations and action plans from the major UN conferences of the last decade. The Summit's

Programme for Further Implementation of Agenda 21 and Commitments to the Rio Principles focused on the challenge related to setting up achievable targets backed up by adequate resources and transparent monitoring mechanisms.

90. Detailed rules for the implementation of the Protocol, particularly on compliance, reporting, and financial and technological support were discussed in Bonn, Germany (July 2001), and in Marrakesh, Morocco (November 2001). There was a general agreement on the Protocol's implementing mechanisms, which include emissions trading, joint implementation, and investments in clean technologies.

91. Its focus is on the sustainable use of biological diversity with the development of national strategies and a fair sharing of the benefits coming from the utilization of genetic resources. Cartagena Protocol on Biosafety was adopted in 2000 to protect the planet's species and ecosystems from the potential risks posed by genetically modified organisms with the establishment of an agreement procedure that ensures the revelation of full information prior to the import of such organisms.

92. It also created an elaborate series of trade permits within each category of endangered species and between importing and exporting countries. Lacking a provision for sanctions in the case of noncompliance, the convention's weakness lies in ineffective or rare enforcement of restrictions.

93. Despite its potential capacity to serve as a powerful tool for conserving migratory wildlife, only about 40 countries have acceded to the agreement due to its enforcement costs and requirements.

94. UNEP was given a broad coordinating role to oversee the work carried out by other agencies in the areas of ozone depletion. Its role also includes convening numerous ad hoc conferences on specific environmental problems, a typical example being a 1977 scientific meeting on threats to the ozone layer.

95. In collecting further scientific knowledge about the climate and global warming, the WMO has built a long history of collaborative relationships with the International Council of Scientific Unions. The implementation of the World Climate Program (WCP) adopted at the second World Climate Conference in 1990 was supported by UNEP and UNESCO.

96. Global and regional monitoring by the WMO's Climate Observing System enables compiling environmental pollution data. The WMO coordinates activities of the Global Ozone Observing System (as part of the Global Atmospheric Watch System) that measures stratospheric ozone concentrations. The program involves more than 140 national stations that collect, exchange, and analyze data.

97. International organizations receive reports on treaty implementation by states and facilitate independent monitoring and inspection. Administrative secretariats have been created to establish and monitor the detailed protocols of treaties and conventions. For instance, the data on CFC production, trade, and consumption are sent to the Ozone Secretariat.

98. The GEF has served as the largest multilateral financial mechanism of the United Nations Framework Convention on Climate Change (UNFCCC) and the Convention on Biological Diversity.

99. As non-sovereign actors, NGOs enhance social and cultural interactions in a global civil society where decentralized networks of social institutions represent different

interests and values. Business seeks profit while other types of organizations pursue political, social, and cultural goals. In contrast with the roles of economic actors such as multinational corporations, the activities of non-governmental organizations are driven by values, and they act out of felt concerns and other non-selfish reasons.

100. Some groups were directly engaged in financing the creation, expansion, and long-term management of protected areas in the world's biodiversity hotspots. For instance, the Global Conservation Fund focused on creating high-biodiversity wilderness areas and important marine regions (notably, coral reef hotspots) with a $100 million grant from the Gordon and Betty Moore Foundation.

101. Millennium Ecosystem Assessment, *Synthesis Report*, 2005, p. 2. Available online at http://www.millenniumassessment.org.

102. Groombridge, Brian and Martin D. Jenkins, *The World Atlas of Biodiversity.*

103. "A Whole New World," *Kids Discover Earth*, Vol. 14, #3 (March 2004).

104. Queen Noor of Jordan, "The Right to Diversity," *Our Planet*, 2003. Available online at http://www.ourplanet.com.

105. Ibid.

Berinstein, Paula. *Alternative Energy: Facts, Statistics, and Issues.* Westport, CT: Oryx Press, 2001.

Bortman, Marci, et al., eds. *Environmental Encyclopaedia*, Vol. 1. Detroit: Thomas Gale Publishing, 2003.

Bowles, Ian A., and Prickett, Glenn, eds. *Footprints in the Jungle: Natural Resource Industries, Infrastructure, and Biodiversity Conservation.* New York: Oxford University Press, 2001.

Brown, R. Lester. *Eco-Economy: Building an Economy for the Earth.* New York: W. W. Norton & Company, 2001.

Chambers, Nicky, Craig Simmons, and Mathis Wackernagel. *Sharing Nature's Interest: Ecological Footprints as an Indicator of Sustainability.* Sterling, VA: Earthscan Publishing, 2000.

Collier, Michael, and Robert Webb. *Floods, Droughts, and Climate Change.* Tucson, AZ: University of Arizona Press, 2002.

Doherty, Brian. *Ideas and Actions in the Green Movement.* London: Routledge, 2002.

Dowswell, Elizabeth. "Production and Consumption," *Our Planet.* Available online at http://www.ourplanet.com.

Evans, Kim Masters. *Garbage and Other Pollution.* Farmington Hills, MI: Thompson Gale, 2004.

Environmental Protection Agency. *Municipal Solid Waste in the US: 2001 Facts and Figures.* Available online at www.epa.org.

Gardner, Gary, et al. "The State of Consumption Today." In Worldwatch Institute, *State of the World.* New York: W. W. Norton & Company, 2004, pp. 3–21.

Global Footprint Network, *Humanity's Footprint 1961–2001.* Available online at http://www.footprintnetwork.org.

Good, Leonard. 'Brightening the Future', *Our Planet.* Available online at http://www.ourplanet.com.

Griffin, J. *Global Climate Change.* UK: Edward Elgar Publishing, 2003.

Groombridge, Brian, and Jenkins, Martin D. *The World Atlas of Biodiversity: Earth's Living Resources in the 21st Century.* Los Angeles: University of California Press. 2002.

Harrison, Paul, and Fred Pearce. *Atlas of Population and Environment.* Los Angeles: University of California Press and American Association for the Advancement of Science, 2001.

Ludwig, Christian, et al. *Municipal Solid Waste Management.* Berlin: Springer, 2003.

Makower, Joel, and Deborah Fleischer. *Sustainable Consumption and Production: Strategies for Accelerating Positive Change.* New York: Environmental Grantmakers Association, 2003.

Martens, William Jozef, and P. Martens. *Environmental Change, Climate and Health: Issues and Research Methods.* Cambridge: Cambridge University Press, 2002.

McCarthy, James, et al., eds. *Climate Change: Impacts, Adaptation and Vulnerability: Contribution of Working Group II to the Third Assessment Report of IPCC.* Cambridge, MA: Cambridge University Press.

Meadows, Donella, et al. *Limits to Growth: The 30-Year Update.* Chelsea Green Publishing, 2004.

Messiaen, Maarten. "Environment: Global North's 'Ecological Footprint' Dwarfs South's." Global Information Network, October 22, 2004. Available online at http://www.globalinfo.org.

Munn, Ted, and Ian Douglas. *Encyclopedia of Global Environmental Change.* New York: John Wiley and Sons, 2002.

National Geographic, "The End of Cheap Oil." (June 2004).

Novacek, Michael, ed. *The Biodiversity Crisis: Losing What Counts.* New York: New Press, 2001.

O'Keefe, P. "Biomass Burning in Rural Homes in Tropical Areas" in *Encyclopaedia of Global Environmental Change.* John Wiley and Sons Publishing, 2002.

Pew Center. *Global Climate Change.* Arlington, VA: 2004. Available online at www.pewclimate.org.

Rainforestweb.org. "World Rainforest Information Portal," 2001. Available online at http://www.rainforestweb.org/Rainforest_Information/ Biodiversity.

Rainforest Action Network. "RAN Annual Report 2003-2004." San Francisco, CA. Available online at http://www.ran.org.

Ravindranath, Nijavalli H., and Sathaye, Jayant. *Climate Change and Developing Countries.* Netherlands: Kluiver Academic Publishers, 2002.

Redefining Progress. "Ecological Footprint Analysis." 1994–2004, Oakland, CA. Available online at http://www.rprogress.org.

Reid, Walter V., et al., "Millennium Ecosystem Assessment Synthesis Report." Millennium Ecosystem Assessment, 2005. Available online at http://www.millenniumassessment.org.

Reynolds, J., N. Dulvy, and C. Roberts. "Exploitation and Other Threats to Fish Conservation." In P. Hart and J. Reynolds, eds. *Handbook of Fish Biology and Fisheries,* Vol. 2. Oxford: Blackwell Publishing, 2002.

Rischard, Jean-Francois F. *High Noon: 20 Global Problems, 20 Years to Solve Them.* New York: Basic Books, 2002.

Sawin, Janet L. "Making Better Energy Choices." In Worldwatch Institute, *State of the World.* New York: W. W. Norton & Company, 2004, pp. 24–43.

Spalding, M., C. Ravilious, and E. Green. *The World Atlas of Coral Reefs.* Los Angeles: University of California Press, 2001.

Speth, James Gustave. *Red Sky at Morning: America and the Crisis of the Global Environment.* New Haven: Yale University Press, 2004.

Spray, S. and K.L. McGlothin. *Global Climate Change.* New York: Rowman and Littlefield Publishing Inc, 2002.

Toepfer, Klaus. "At a Glance: Waste," *Our Planet.* Available online at http://www.ourplanet.com.

Trenberth, Kevin, et al. *Effects of Changing Climate on Weather and Human Activities.* Sausalito, CA: University Science Books, 2000.

U.S. Census Bureau. *Global Population Profile 2002.* Available online atwww.census.gov/ipc/www/wp02.html.

UNEP, UNICEF, and WHO. *Children in the New Millennium: Environmental Impact on Health.* Available online at www.unep.org.

UNEP, UNDP, The World Bank, and World Resources Institute. *2002–2004 World Resources: Decisions for the Earth.* Washington D.C.: World Resource Institute, 2003.

UNEP. *Global Environmental Outlook-3 (GEO-3).* Earthscan/James & James, 2004.

UNEP. *Improving Municipal Wastewater Management in Coastal Cities: A Training Manual.* Available online at http://www.gpa.unep.org/training.

UNESCO. *International Year of Fresh Water: Facts and Figures: Desertification and Drought.* Available online at http://www.wateryear2003.org.

van Ierland, E.C., et al., eds. *Issues in International Climate Policy.* Chettenham, UK: Edward Elgar Press, 2003.

Vigil, Kenneth M. *Clean Water: An Introduction to Water Quality and Water Pollution Control,* 2nd ed. Corvallis, OR: Oregon State University Press, 2003.

Ward, Diane Raines. *Water Wars.* New York: Riverhead Books, 2002.

Weart, Spencer R. *The Discovery of Global Warming.* Cambridge: Harvard University Press, 2003.

Wood, Charles, and Porro, Robert, eds. *Deforestation and Land Use in the Amazon.* Gainesville, FL: University Press of Florida, 2002.

World Bank. *World Development Report 2004.* Washington D.C.: World Bank and Oxford University Press, 2004.

World Wildlife Fund. *Living Planet Report 2004.* Gland, Switzerland: WWF, 2004.

BIBLIOGRAPHY

Worldwatch Institute. *State of the World.* New York: W. W. Norton & Company, 2004.

Worldwatch Institute. *Vital Signs: The Trends That Are Shaping Our Future.* New York: W. W. Norton & Company, 2003.

Barbour, Scott. *The Environment.* San Diego, CA: Greenhaven Press, 2000.

Burnie, David. *Endangered Planet.* Boston: Kingfisher, 2004.

Chiras, Daniel D. *The New Ecological Home: A Complete Guide to Green Building*

Options. White River Junction, VT: Chelsea Green Publishing, 2004.

Dalgleish, Sharon. *Our World Our Future: Protecting Forests.* Philadelphia, PA: Chelsea House Publishers, 2002.

Dalgleish, Sharon. *Our World Our Future: Managing the Land.* Philadelphia, PA: Chelsea House Publishers, 2002.

Donald, Rhonda Lucas. *Endangered Animals.* Danbury CT: Scholastic (Children's Press), 2001.

Gerdes, Louise I., ed. *Endangered Oceans.* San Diego: Greenhaven Press, 2004.

Hohm, Charles F. *Population.* San Diego, CA: Greenhaven Press, 2000.

Knight, Tim. *Journey into the Rainforest.* New York: Oxford University Press, 2001.

Lansky, Mitch. *Low-Impact Forestry: Forestry as if the Future Mattered.* Maine: Environmental Policy Institute, 2003.

Maass, Robert. *Garbage.* New York: Henry Holt, 2000.

McDonough, William, and Michael Braungart. *Cradle to Cradle: Remaking the Way We Make Things.* New York: North Point Press, 2002.

McKee, Jeffrey Kevin. *Sparing nature : the conflict between human population growth and earth's biodiversity,* N.J.: Rutgers University Press, 2003.

McKibben, Bill. *The End of Nature.* New York: Anchor Books, 1990.

Mongillo, John F. *Teen Guides to Environmental Science.* Westport, CT: Greenwood Press, 2004.

Nagel, Stuart S. *Environmental Policy and Developing Nations,* Jefferson, NC: McFarland, 2002.

Newman, Arnold. *Tropical Rainforest.* New York: Checkmark Books, 2002.

Parks, Peggy J. *Global Warming.* San Diego, CA: Lucent Books, 2004.

Redefining Progress, Ecological Footprint Quiz. Available online at http://www.earthday.net/footprint/index.asp.

United Nations Environmental Programme, *Tunza: The UNEP Magazine for Youth.* Available online at http://www.ourplanet.com/tunza.

UNEP. *Pachamama: Our Earth, Our Future.* Available online at http://www.unep.org.

Raven, Peter H., Linda R. Berg, and John V. Aliff. *Environment,* 4th Edition. Wiley Publishing.

Vogel, Carole Garbuny. *Human Impact,* New York: F. Watts, 2003.

PICTURE CREDITS

Ho-Won Jeong is a faculty member at the Institute for Conflict Analysis and Resolution at George Mason University. He is passionate about the natural world and its preservation. He has written a book entitled *Global Environmental Policymaking* (2001), as well as journal and encyclopedia articles on deforestation, wildlife preservation, the rain forests, and environmental values. He hopes to build a vision for a sustainable future with environmental education.

James Bacchus is Chairman of the Global Trade Practice Group of the international law firm Greenberg Traurig, Professional Association. He is also a visiting professor of international law at Vanderbilt University Law School. He served previously as a special assistant to the United States Trade Representative; as a Member of the Congress of the United States, from Florida; and as a Member, for eight years, and Chairman, for two terms, of the Appellate Body of the World Trade Organization. His book, *Trade and Freedom*, was published by Cameron May in London in 2004, and is now in its third edition worldwide.

Ilan Alon, Ph.D., is Associate Professor of International Business at the Crummer Graduate School of Business of Rollins College. He holds a Ph.D in International Business and Economics from Kent State University. He currently teaches courses on Business in the Global Environment and Emerging Markets: China in the business curriculum as well as International Trade and Economics in the economics curriculum.

DATE DUE